THEORY AND PRACTICE IN EDUCATION

THEORY AND PRACTICE IN EDUCATION

R.F. Dearden

ROUTLEDGE & KEGAN PAUL
London, Boston, Melbourne and Henley

This collection first published in 1984 by
Routledge & Kegan Paul plc
39 Store Street, London WC1E 7DD,
9 Park Street, Boston, Mass. 02108, USA,
464 St Kilda Road, Melbourne,
Victoria 3004, Australia and
Broadway House, Newtown Road,
Henley-on-Thames, Oxon RG9 1EN.
Printed by Billing & Sons Ltd, Worcester
Chapter 1 © University of Birmingham 1979
Chapter 2 © Basil Blackwell 1982
Chapter 3 © R.F. Dearden 1983
Chapter 4 © Philosophy of Education Society of Great Britain
          1980
Chapter 5 © R.F. Dearden 1981
Chapter 6 © Journals Oxford Ltd 1980
Chapter 7 © Taylor & Francis Ltd 1980
Chapter 8 © Basil Blackwell 1974
Chapter 9 © R.F. Dearden 1982
Chapter 10 © Basil Blackwell 1979
Chapter 11 © Educational Review 1981
Chapter 12 © R.F. Dearden 1978
Chapter 13 © Colin Richards 1980
This collection © R.F. Dearden 1984

Library of Congress Cataloging in Publication Data

Dearden, R.F.
Theory and practice in education.
Includes index.
1. Education -- Philosophy -- Addresses, essays, lectures.
2. Teaching -- Addresses, essays, lectures. 3. Learning --
Addresses, essays, lectures. 4. Education and state --
Addresses, essays, lectures. I. Title.
LB880.D4T48 1983   370'.1   83-10977

ISBN 0-7100-9910-X

CONTENTS

ACKNOWLEDGMENTS

I am grateful to the editors and publishers who have granted permission to use material previously published in their books and journals.   Chapter 1 was first published by the University of Birmingham.   Chapter 2 appeared in the 'British Jour-Journal of Educational Studies', vol. XXX, no. 1, February 1982.   Chapter 3 is previously unpublished.   Chapter 4 appeared in the 'Journal of Philosophy of Education', vol. 14, no. 2, 1980.   Chapter 5 was first published by the 'Cambridge Journal of Education', vol. 11, no. 2, Easter 1981. Chapter 6 was first published by the 'Oxford Review of Education', vol. 6, no. 3, 1980.   Chapter 7 appeared in the 'Journal of Curriculum Studies', vol. 13, no. 1, 1981.   Chapter 8 first appeared in the 'British Journal of Educational Studies', vol. XXII, no. 1, February 1974.   Chapter 9 was the Froebel bicentenary lecture given at the Froebel Institute College in 1982.   Chapter 10 was first published by the 'British Journal of Educational Studies', vol. XXVII, no. 2, 1979.   Chapter 11 was first published in 'The Behaviourist in the Classroom', ed. Kevin Wheldall, Educational Review Offset Publications no. 1, 1981.   Chapter 12 was first published in 'Education 3-13', vol. 6, no. 1, April 1978.   Chapter 13 first appeared in 'Primary Education: Issues for the Eighties', ed. Colin Richards, A. & C. Black, 1980.

INTRODUCTION

The thirteen papers which constitute the present collection
were each written for a separate occasion and can consequent-
ly be read quite independently of each other.   Nevertheless,
the grouping of them into four parts is not arbitrary.   It
draws attention to a degree of community of theme and what
is mentioned only in passing in one is often taken up and
developed in a following paper.

In a very general sense every one of these papers could be
said to be about the relation of theory to practice in education, but that relation is the especial concern of the first,
from which the collection as a whole takes its title.   Various
strategies may be adopted by new professors in giving their
inaugural lectures but my own chosen one in this piece was to
review the state of educational theory.   I tried to character-
ise its nature, considered the notion of 'application' as it
applies to educational theory and concluded with some comments on justification.   The topic is one on which any philosopher of education should be ready to declare himself on
account of its generality of bearing, its perennial interest and
indeed its political urgency.

Chapters two to four continue with this self-consciousness
about theory.   Philosophy of education as just one of the
educational disciplines is the particular concern of chapter two.
This piece was commissioned by the editor of the 'British Journal of Educational Studies' as a contribution to a special issue
commemorative of thirty years of the journal, hence its title.
I was grateful for the challenge that this occasion provided to
review the evolution of the discipline over a period in which it
has undergone fundamental changes.   I see no reason now to
wish to modify the sombre look into the future with which I
ended that piece, and indeed the only editorial emendation that
I have made for the present collection is to omit the first two
paragraphs of the original article since they related rather specifically to the commemorative occasion.

Chapter three was written for a very strange conference in
Naples which, through some organisational problems, still had
not taken place at the time that this collection was put
together.   The theme of the conference was a somewhat European concern which falls strangely on British ears, namely the

'science of pedagogy'.   The general idea seemed to be that
we had now reached the point when some kind of unified science of education might be possible if only we would all bend
our efforts to it.   I doubted whether such a project could be
carried through, even in principle, and this short piece articulated the grounds for my scepticism.   The only possibility
which I saw for any such unified science was for the Gordian
knot to be cut by a political decision, though that would be
intellectually arbitrary.

The relationship of education to politics was, however, the
explicit focus for chapter four.   Two circumstances gave rise
to this piece.   The first was the growing prominence of arguments and policy statements which claimed or implied that the
state should have control, or at least should have more control, over the curriculum.   The second was the in many ways
closely analogous debate that occurs in considering the relation of politics to sport, for instance in connection with the
1980 Olympic Games.   The piece that I wrote was concerned
primarily with the question of whether education could be,
rather than ought to be, kept out of politics.   I concluded
that it could not, but that did not carry with it any direct
implication that state control of the curriculum was justified.

Part two concerns the curriculum but contains no grand
design or overall prescription for curriculum construction.
The occasion for the chapter on balance and coherence was a
conference of people who were mainly concerned with philosophy of education but who were also concerned about the spate
of reports which had recently issued from the DES and the
Inspectorate.   It was rightly felt that philosophers of education should give some attention to influential policy documents
such as these, as well as to discussing more perennial but
abstract themes.   In many ways what resulted by way of my
own contribution was akin to a piece on needs which I had
written in 1966.   It seemed to me that although the terms had
changed the ambiguities and their political significance were
much the same.

The piece on general education is a contribution to the philosophical debate which is usually conducted under the title
'general powers of the mind', a form of words given currency
by Paul Hirst in connection with his forms of knowledge thesis.
It seemed to me that this theme, which in many ways is a re-
incarnation of yesterday's preoccupation with transfer of training in psychology, was re-emerging strongly both in recent
official reports and in more academic writing.   To my own sur-
prise, I concluded that there could well be something in it and
that at least some general powers might well be possible,
though they could never be sufficient in any particular employment.   What seemed to have been overlooked was that although,

as Hirst had strongly argued, any such general power as problem-solving ability could never be sufficient by itself, it nevertheless did not follow that there could be nothing general. Even if this is true, however, the hope seems excessively over-optimistic that general powers could provide a complete answer to the problems of expansion and obsolescence in knowledge. A man for all seasons would need more, much more, than any general powers could equip him with.

Lawrence Stenhouse's Humanities Curriculum Project has excited philosophical interest ever since it was launched in 1970. Like other philosophers of education, I have felt considerable sympathetic attraction to it but also some serious critical reservations. Chapter seven represents my own coming to terms with the problem of controversial issues in the curriculum and with Stenhouse's principle of procedural neutrality. In general what I did was to suggest a strengthening of his case for the inclusion of controversial material in the curriculum but at the same time I raised doubts about the centrality of the principle of procedural neutrality, and even about whether it deserved to be called a principle at all.

Autonomy has been a major preoccupation of mine since I wrote my 'Philosophy of Primary Education' (Routledge & Kegan Paul, 1968). It was also the subject of my doctoral dissertation. In various ways this preoccupation surfaces in all four of the chapters which constitute part three. Chapter eight, on the ethics of belief, is the earliest article (1974) contained in the present collection and I reprint it now partly because I see no reason to change it and partly because it seems to me that its theme has never been sufficiently discussed. The principal point that I tried to argue in the piece was that although the assessment of belief is a logical or epistemic matter, nevertheless to engage in such assessment rather than to have one's beliefs determined in one of many other ways was itself a choice which had ethical significance. Intellectual education is a matter not just of becoming familiar with certain content, or even of practising certain skills, but is in an important way a development of character. Associated with missing this aspect of intellectual activity is a model of the mind as an organ for seeing, which conceals the fact that true belief (or at any rate tested belief) is often won only by a struggle. Though I did not mention it in the article, a related teaching problem which had puzzled me for years was that of the frequent inadequacy of clarity of explanation by itself to modify learners.

An invitation from the Froebel Institute to contribute one of a series of Froebel bicentenary lectures on the subject of autonomy gave an opportunity to return to this topic. The occasion explains the early section in the article in which I

relate autonomy to child-centred education. But the nature
of intellectual education took precedence over autonomy as the
main explicit theme, though I argued that the two are closely
connected in various ways. The theme of the ethics of belief
was raised again and I took the opportunity to relate intellectual education not only to character but also to imagination
and emotion, on which topics I have always felt especially
benefitted by the work of R.K. Elliott and Richard Peters.

With the exception of an article by Antony Flew which I
mention in chapter ten, the assessment of learning is a topic
which has largely escaped philosophical attention, though one
would have expected epistemology and philosophy of mind to
have much to say about it. I took the opportunity in the
article on this topic to consider some of the epistemic hazards
that accompany assessment, the possibility of objectivity in
assessing and the place of comparisons in framing judgements
about learners.

Behaviourism is a theme on which I touch in several places,
for example in chapters one, eight and ten, but behaviour
modification is the major concern of chapter eleven. This
paper was included in a collection of fourteen articles entitled
'The Behaviourist in the Classroom', edited by Kevin Wheldall
(Educational Review Offset Publications No. 1, University of
Birmingham, 1981). The collection largely consisted of statements by enthusiasts for behaviour modification, so that my
own reservations represented one of the few voices of dissent,
or at least caution. Richard Peters had long ago taught me
that the main problem with behaviourism was its concept of
behaviour, and I applied this judgement in the article. In
the course of preliminary reading I was struck, however, by
the lack of theoretical unity of commitment amongst practitioners of and propagandists for behaviour modification. They
seemed to me to vary from pure Skinnerians to people who
were behaviourists in little more than being unusually systematic about their use of ordinary encouragement and discouragement. I am myself convinced, however, that this issue is one
of the most important to get right in any educational connection.

The final two articles both relate to primary education and
were written with non-specialist audiences and readers in
mind. 'Reflections on Plowden' was my contribution to a
series on the theme 'Plowden ten years on' which appeared in
the journal 'Education 3-13' during 1978. The Plowden Report
had itself called for a review after ten years, though with the
implication that it would be progress towards Plowden objectives that would be assessed. The primary survey, 'Primary
Education in England' (HMSO, 1978), was the Inspectorate's
own assessment after ten years, and chapter thirteen in the

present collection is my own comment on that survey.   It was in the course of reading that survey, together with certain other official reports, that I became convinced that general powers of the mind (the theme of chapter six) were making something of a comeback.   The 'Oxford Review' article now reprinted as chapter six was a later and more academic treatment of this theme.

I have indicated in this introduction something of the circumstances surrounding the writing of these various papers, not (I hope) from any vain pleasure in autobiography, still less to provide fodder for some sociologists of knowledge, but in the belief that contextual knowledge of such circumstances often helps in understanding what is actually being said. There is an academic tradition which requires as much as possible of oneself to be kept out of what one writes, but it may be questioned whether that tradition is entirely helpful. Pure philosophers range from those, like Spinoza, who conceal everything of themselves to those (I refrain from examples) who write about nothing but themselves.   But when a species of theorising is intended to have a bearing on practice, it must surely be relevant to indicate something of the practical concerns and associated statements of policy which occasioned the theorising.   Above all this must be true when the relation of theory to practice is one of the themes that is explicitly being discussed.

Part one
THEORY AND PRACTICE

1 THEORY AND PRACTICE IN EDUCATION

I

The public reception given to a piece of educational research is commonly a function only partly of the research itself, or of its intrinsic interest.   In part it will also be a function of the political climate surrounding its publication.   Published at one time, and the research may attract little or no attention;   published at another and its author is instantly elevated into being a 'teleperson' and 'jet-setter'.   Quite as curious is the rise and fall in popularity of the various general branches of educational study.   Thus the traditionally well-entrenched educational studies of psychology and of history were for a time outshone, first by philosophy and then by sociology.   These in turn were displaced from pre-eminence by curriculum studies, while the most recent candidate for the role of quasi-messianic leadership is the study of management. Each in turn waxes and then wanes, outshone by some newly rising star.   I shall resist the temptation to speculate on the possible identity of the next new luminary.

Across these fluctuations, however, it is possible to discern a movement of longer span.   I refer to the rise and fall in popularity of theoretical studies as a whole.   These rose rapidly in esteem during the early 1960s, encouraged no doubt by the Robbins Report of 1963 with its suggestion that there should be a degree in educational studies, the BEd as it came to be called, and with its suggestion that the colleges were too narrowly conceived as places only of training.   Also at this time some very influential articles were published on the nature of educational theory and its relations to practice.   For example, Richard Peters persuasively argued for an ending to what he provocatively called 'undifferentiated mush', and for its replacement by studies firmly grounded in the separate theoretical disciplines, such as history, psychology, sociology and philosophy, to name the four that became canonical. (1) Major series of student texts were published under the eye of general editors whose appointments intentionally fell within these divisions.   And, perhaps for the first time, a major government report on some aspect of education, the Plowden Report of 1967 on primary education, rested heavily on evidence and perspectives drawn from theory.   In the second half of the 1960s, theory was riding high.

But with the 1970s has come something of a downswing, and
not simply for reasons of cost-cutting or the demoralising
closure of colleges.   There have been grumbles that in the
enthusiasm for theory too much attention has been distracted
from practical preparation for the classroom.   By 1972, the
James Report was already demoting theory in its proposed
second cycle of professional preparation.   More recently, the
schools have been criticised for being too readily wooed by
'theorists', who are apparently envisaged as a band of peripa-
tetic half-wits, too fleet of foot ever actually to be seen.
Some politicians, especially some noisy ones on the right, regularly promise to take a hatchet to theory if only we will place
political power in their firmly practical hands.

Complaints of these kinds are not wholly new.   No doubt
they have their corrective place in the general scheme of
things.   But what is arguably new is a degree of disenchantment with theory amongst some theorists themselves.   As
early as 1957, Professor D.J. O'Connor had deprecatingly referred to the term 'educational theory' as being no more than
a 'courtesy title', but this remark was swept aside in the general mood of rising optimism. (2)   By 1975, however, John
Wilson could write a whole book raising doubts both about the
benefits of theory and, more radically, about whether educational theory actually existed at all in any reputable form. (3)
In 1976, Hartnett and Naish, generously granted the space of
two volumes by their publishers, remained at the close uncon-
vinced of the relevance of theory. (4)   Other theorists, perhaps thinking that professional suicide would be the only hon-
ourable course if these doubts were well founded, have turned
to commonsense, not so much to exhibit some as to make of it
a last remaining object of legitimate study, although no doubt
in due course one to be made into something learned and
obscure.

So what are we to think of theory?   Was its general rise to
prominence just a strange and temporary aberration for the
sturdily pragmatic British?   The teachers themselves commonly
regard theory with a varying mixture of respect and suspicion:
respect because it is thought of as difficult, and suspicion
because its bearings are unclear on the detailed decision as to
what to do next Monday morning.   But is that suspicion
grounded in the right expectations?   Detailed practical assis-
tance was never promised in the programmatic outlines of the
1960s.   For Richard Peters, what philosophy was to offer was
only a gradual change of perspective. (5)   Brian Simon blunt-
ly said that 'no claim should be made that the study of history
of education directly affects the practice of the teacher in the
classroom'. (6)   William Taylor added that 'the justification
for the inclusion of sociological studies in the course for intending teachers does not rest on any observable link between

the pursuit of such studies and the improvement of classroom
technique or practice'. (7)

One possible explanation of the disenchantment with theory
is therefore that it has come to be regarded with inappropriate
expectations.   In consequence, it is judged to be failing
where it could not succeed.   Where initial training is concern-
ned, the traditional disfavour of theory might, at least to some
extent, be attributed to the natural impatience of beginners to
be up and doing in the practical roles for which they have
cast themselves.   Apparently even doctors in training show
some impatience with their early theoretical studies of anatomy,
physiology and biochemistry.   Indeed, the relation between
theory and practice causes puzzlement across a very wide field.
How is economics related to running a business, jurisprudence
to being a lawyer, theology to faith, ethics to conduct, logic
to reasoning, or, for that matter, sociology to being a police
inspector?   Different subject-matters will no doubt yield somewhat different answers, but not to the extent of precluding
some striking parallels between them all.

To cut a long introduction short, it seems timely to look
once again at the nature of educational theory and its relations
to practice.   The problems so raised are problems both for
theory and for practice.   They are problems for practice if
we are trying to decide what sort of theory to teach, how
much, in what way, to whom, where and when, or if we are
preoccupied with the different sets of answers that might be
appropriate in initial by contrast with in-service training.
But they are problems for theory if we are concerned more
abstractly to enquire into the nature of educational theory
itself, or the sense in which it could be expected to be relevant to practice.   It is primarily with these theoretical questions that I shall be concerned.   Discussing them will involve
some boundary-crossing references to many branches of educational studies, but the questions themselves fall largely within
the philosophy of education, as being especially concerned with
a scrutiny of the forms and interconnections of certain sorts of
knowledge.

II

What meaning, then, can be attached to the term 'theory' in
education?   There is more than one answer available.   Quite
often what is meant is simply an idea that is impractical.
Thus someone full of enthusiasm for de-schooling as an idea
might suggest using the city as a school, with scant regard
for the fact that the weather is quite often cold and wet.   As
James McClellan laconically remarks, one thing that we can say
about school is that it beats standing out in the rain;   or

consider the student who plans a fine lesson on the onion
(fine 'in theory' that is), only to find his classroom transformed into a gas chamber within minutes of the children's first
inquisitive incisions.   This first sense of 'theory' points to
the many occasions when we wish to distinguish theoretical
from practical possibility, a distinction to which I shall later
return.

Again, sometimes what is meant by 'theory' is knowledge
that may be admirable as far as it goes, such as propositional
knowledge of valid general principles, but the possessor of
which is as yet untried in practice.   He knows, in a propositional way, such things as that one should start from the
known, that one should build on existing interests, that one
should avoid relying on extrinsic motivation, or that one
should present material as the solution to some problem, but it
is uncertain how far he will be capable of the detailed judgement, and the coping with the unpredictable, which the valid
'application' of these principles will bring.   Plato's picture of
the philosopher who has beheld the Sun, but who at first
blunders about when he re-enters the cave of ordinary experience, provides a graphic image of the problems here.   Doubtless every profession has in its folklore versions of the story
of the teacher full of theoretical knowledge in this sense, and
always a graduate, who is tripped by his first encounter with
Joe Bloggs in 3C.

Less prejudicial and more fundamental is the distinction
between theory and practice which contrasts questions as to
what is the case with questions as to what should be done, or
factual assertions about how things are with value-judgements
bearing on how to act.   Thus the theorist Lawrence Kohlberg
may tell us how moral development proceeds through a certain
invariable sequence, whereas what guides the moral agent is a
particular code or set of principles.   But should we concur
here in the tacit assumption that evaluative or practical judgements are not also statements of what is the case, so perhaps
granting at the very start a non-cognitivist theory of ethics?
On the other hand, are all of the envisaged factual assertions
really to be called 'theoretical'?   Is the assertion 'this is a
blackboard duster' to be classed as theoretical, as it would
have to be on the suggested ground of distinction?

What is already clear, I think, is that the distinction between
theory and practice is not just one distinction but a shifting
set of contrasts made to serve different, although possibly
equally valid, purposes.   Just as we use the term 'belief'
sometimes to include and sometimes to exclude knowledge, so
may theory sometimes cover everyday assertions of commonsense but at other times contrast with commonsense a more
abstract and systematised understanding.   Factual surveys

and reports, such as the recent report of the inspectorate
'Primary Education in England', fall somewhat indeterminately
in this shifting borderline area.   For example, is the statement theoretical or practical that 17 per cent of the schools
which could stream their 11-year-olds now actually do so?

A classic debate on this topic is that between D.J. O'Connor
and Paul Hirst. (8)   For O'Connor, science provided the
paradigm of theory, which he defined as 'a logically connected
set of hypotheses whose main function is to explain their subject matter'.   In tough positivist fashion he then saw psychology and sociology as offering the principal hope of some
genuine educational theory.   But even here he expected most
of what is useful to be only commonsense, since we are not
strangers to human nature and since teaching is no new endeavour.   Even on this limited account, however, something
more might be said in favour of theory.   By its testing of
truth it might transform a commonsense impression into relia-
able hard fact;   by its jargon it might effect a very useful
economy of expression for a familiar enough idea, as with the
concept of the 'self-fulfilling prophecy';   and all this is quite
apart from the fact that what ought to be commonsense is not
always so common.

But these points of detail apart, Hirst's much more radical
reply to O'Connor was that, in adopting a scientific paradigm,
he completely misconceived the nature of educational theory.
Better analogies, if justice is to be done, are to be found in
such practical but theoretically informed pursuits as engineering, politics and medicine.   That is to say, 'theory' must be
seen as referring to general practical principles which are justified by reference to their backing in various disciplines.
Elaborating on this a little, we may expect that the term 'educational theory' will sometimes refer to principles, sometimes to
backing, and sometimes to both.   Plato's educational theorising is a good example of the more comprehensive use of the
term.

Hirst further adds that the transition from backing to practical principles is never a simple deductive step.   No doubt
he has in mind here some familiar although not uncontested
points about the so-called 'naturalistic fallacy', such as that
facts never speak for themselves, or that by themselves facts
are without practical force or bearing.   A 'practical' theory,
as he would prefer to call educational and other such theories,
must include values in order to give practical guidance or to
have practical relevance.

O'Connor seems to accept the possibility of there being such
a class of 'practical theories', but he rejects Hirst's evident
assumption that educational theory will be monolithic.   The

incorporation of values brings with it, in his view, disagreements for which there is no shared or agreed decision-procedure.   Thus some people will favour specialisation in the sixth form and others a more general education;   some will favour competition and others intrinsic motivation;   some will assess comprehensive education only by its examination results, while others will look for gains in social cohesion, equality of opportunity, or the acquisition of a common culture.   Package deals, such as Plato's, Rousseau's or Dewey's educational theories, are therefore inherently controversial.

Accepting something from both O'Connor and Hirst in this debate, I would myself want to say that educational theory is the product of a particular endeavour, namely the endeavour to achieve an intellectually deepened understanding of educational practice in all its aspects: both curricular and institutional, and both empirical and evaluative.   But to speak of a 'deeper' understanding is of course to rely on an unexplained metaphor, and moreover it is to suggest a line of division where none can in fact be drawn.   Suppose a shrewd headteacher, contemplating with dismay his falling roll, thinks this problem through to the point where he sees that he must make his school more attractive to the parents of a dwindling number of children.   Has he then started to theorise?   If not, then suppose him to go one step further and to see the likely consequences, especially if this trend is widely distributed, of a shift in the control of schools towards more parental influence. Surely by now he is theorising?   Yet where was there a boundary to cross?

While it may be impossible to give clear necessary and sufficient conditions for theory, nevertheless typical illustrations can be given of the sort of thing that one has in mind. Theorising typically involves such activities as the careful testing of truth, either by critical argument or by empirical research.   To assist in this, it typically makes careful distinctions, sets up hypotheses, teases out assumptions, assesses validity, reveals presuppositions, scrutinises justifications and explores alternative interpretations or frameworks.   It searches for a basis in general principle and examines what lies behind such principles.   Something remains in all this of the Greek origins of the term, for in theorising we seek as it were to gaze upon the reality behind the appearances, freed both from the particularity and from the importunity of practice.   Whatever the origins of any branch of theory in practice, its theorists soon become reluctant to be simple handmaidens, in part because their theoretical activity comes to be governed by its own autonomous standards of excellence. Thus educational theorists are drawn from the question of what to do next Monday morning to more general inquiries into such questions as how exactly language is acquired, what conception of knowledge is presupposed by curriculum integration, how teacher labelling affects a child's self-concept, whether education redresses social inequality at all, why some children fail to learn certain things, and so on.

A chicken-and-egg problem lies in the direction in which I am gesturing here.   If I begin by defining educational theory as the product of an endeavour to understand educational practice, does this whole approach not presuppose a satisfactory identification of educational practice in the first place? For such an identification of specifically *educational* practice can hardly be accomplished by so simple a device as pointing to what goes on in schools.   Much that goes on in schools is not educational at all, while something of what goes on outside them is.   Must we not therefore first have a theoretical concept of what may distinctively count as 'educational' before we can be in a position to identify the relevant practice, with the result that my account of theory is circular from the start? That is, educational theory would be the result of an endeavour to understand that practice which theory itself must first pick out as educational.   Thus which comes first, chicken or egg?

Provided that we take this, not as a question about abstract logical relationships, but as a question about certain historically evolving activities, then I do not think that we have to choose.   Neither theory nor practice will then have any general priority, but rather they will exist in mutually modificatory tension, as happens wherever an evolving human practice endeavours to understand itself.   The nature of the rings around Saturn will not be altered simply by the attempt to understand them, but the nature of a school or university may well be altered in and by the attempt to understand it. Where we are both participants and observers, the attempt to understand both modifies, and is modified by, practice.

The broad characterisation of educational theory which I have suggested yields a distinction which usefully clarifies the possible relevance of theory to practice.   I will mark this distinction as being between 'thematic' and 'pragmatic' relevance.   By 'thematic' relevance I mean that theory should quite simply be about practice: somewhere or at some time. In this sense, it is a necessary truth that educational theory is relevant to educational practice, although this is not of course to provide a conceptual guarantee that anyone who occupies the role of educational theorist can safely be assumed to be at work on something relevant, any more than having someone in the role of workman guarantees that any work will be done.

By 'pragmatic' relevance, in contrast, I mean having a bearing on the solution of a current practical problem.   Clearly 'thematic' relevance is the wider notion and 'pragmatic' relevance is the sub-class.   In terms of 'thematic' relevance, the child-rearing practices of Samoans, the teaching methods of the Greek Sophists, Herbart's instructional strategies and the metaphysical ideas behind Froebel's gifts are all relevant to educational practice.   But none of them would have any 'pragmatic' relevance for, say, a course on current problems for PGCE students.   The distinction could be a crucial one if educational studies grew from its present modest provision of courses for non-practitioners until such courses became quite common, as a part of undergraduate studies in general arts for example.

An analogous distinction is fairly commonly drawn in other areas of theoretical study.   In history, for example, a distinction is sometimes made between pure history, which can be about anything in the past, such as the mandarins of Ancient China, and 'practical' history, which is addressed to our current problems, in which case the mandarins would feature only on the condition that they were helpful in understanding Mao, or Peking wall posters. (9)   But either way the criteria of truth remain the same, a point not always appreciated by those pragmatists who manage to conflate truth and usefulness, or truth and having satisfactory consequences.

Although I shall return to the point again later, I want immediately to suggest that it would be very unwise for educational theorising to be entirely governed in its direction of interest by a strict criterion of pragmatic relevance.   And this is not just for the familiar reason that, in many fields, theorising detached from practice has often been later found to have most important, although unanticipated, practical applications.   For example, the laser beam was at first referred to as a solution in search of a problem on account of its having no very evident practical applications.   But quite apart from that point, it is important for theory not to be entirely governed by pragmatic relevance, first, because that would put the purpose or ends of current practice themselves beyond theoretical criticism;   and secondly, because in being so governed by practice, theory could very easily become mere apologetic ideology.   These two points are, of course, closely connected.

III

Granted the general characterisation of theory which I have given, various doubts and even radical scepticism as to the desirability of theory for teachers might then be advanced. For example, it might be said that theoretical considerations may well serve not so much to make practical judgement any easier as to make it more difficult, by revealing a greater complexity in the situation.   There is an analogy here with growth in moral understanding, which may well reveal perplexing problems and predicaments where before everything seemed delightfully simple.   Yet truth, and adequacy of conception, have claims on us which may override simplicity in the one case just as in the other.

Harnett and Naish raise another difficulty, although it is unclear how widely it applies. (10)   They point out that on any particular theoretical question there may not be an agreed view, or else an agreed view is possible only with extensive qualifications.   An adequate assessment of the matter therefore requires an awareness of the 'state of the art', and this is something which, if only for reasons of time, students of theory cannot compass.   They may therefore be taught misleadingly simplified versions of theory which do more harm than good.   Sociological references to class characteristics are a case in point.   To judge from some examination scripts, the work of Bernstein is an example of a theorist who has suffered especially in this way.   Thus 'the working class child', i.e. the majority of children, turns out to be a stunted, mumbling imbecilic troglodyte, while 'the middle-class child' radiates all the virtues.   Various drastic solutions to this problem might be suggested, such as confining theory to an intellectual elite amongst teachers, or producing what the Americans have optimistically called 'teacher-proof materials'. But I would not myself despair so soon of the possibilities of improved dissemination and indeed of good quality popularisation, of which there are instances.

There exists a more philosophical tradition of scepticism regarding the role of theory in relation to practice, a good example of which can be found in Ryle's 'Concept of Mind'. (11) Ryle there attacks the 'intellectualist legend', as he calls it, that practice can be intelligent only if it is preceded by the rehearsal of a relevant bit of theory.   Against this view, Ryle points out that practice historically precedes theory, and that still today there are many intelligent practices for which there is no body of theory.   To illustrate this point, some writers have instanced Socrates as a great teacher who taught without benefit of theory, but this seems to me to be just false;   Socrates had an elaborate theory of learning as reminiscence and his teaching was tailored to that conception. (12) But the general point remains valid, and a better example of practice that is intelligent without benefit of theory might be the writing of plays, an art at which Shakespeare had some success apparently without benefit of theory, and certainly without a diploma.

Two other arguments employed by Ryle are that a person

may be fully possessed of theory yet quite incompetent in
practice, which is undeniable, and that to suppose a universal
priority of theory would involve a regress.   For theorising is
itself an intelligent practice, so that it would itself require
some prior theoretical advice if it is to be intelligently done,
which prior advice would in turn require its bit of prior
theorising, and so on.   An endless vista of row upon row of
backseat drivers thus opens up.

A defective variant of this regress argument is to say that
some teaching must be possible without benefit of theory,
since the teaching of theory itself will lie outside its own
scope.   But this is fallacious, since the teaching of theory
can, and in appropriate cases it should, involve reflexive
application.   A baldly didactic piece of instruction on the
theory and the virtues of discovery methods is not a logical
necessity but a joke.   However, what Ryle's arguments do
not show is that, in particular cases, practice cannot be made
still better with some benefit from theory.   It is certainly
true that some levels of intelligent practice are not possible at
all without theory, such as heart surgery, oil prospecting and
designing aeroplanes.   Indeed, in an increasing number of
cases nowadays theory also historically precedes practice, as
it had to do with walking on the moon.

Against the scepticism of theory which I am considering, it
has also been argued that in fact all teaching rests on theory,
although it is conceded that frequently the theory will be
'implicit' only. (13)   A plausible example would be to say that
all teaching implies some theory of learning.   Testing the
truth of this claim would seem to be also a test of how imaginative one is in thinking up possible theories to justify some
practice.   But in the sense of 'implicit' which is involved
here, many theories would be 'implicit' quite without their
being known to, or being psychologically operative in, the
agent said to be acting in accordance with them.   Yet
although a teacher may be quite unaware of the theories
implicit in his practice, criticism of those theories could nevertheless undermine the rationality of that practice.   Traditions
of teaching have indeed been effectively attacked in this way.
The literature of reform, as Dewey very clearly saw, typically
makes extensive use of theoretical considerations both in criticism of tradition and in justification of its own innovative
recommendations. (14)

There is another way in which even a teacher who disavows
any awareness of theory, or use for it, may be closer to it
than he thinks.   It can be embedded and operative in his
practice as a deposit of habit left by his early training, and
now beyond conscious recall.   He cannot now bring to mind
the once received doctrines on fixity of IQ, span of attention,

or the necessity of frequent changes of activity for young children which formed his present practices and habits. It may take a historian of teacher training to elicit such elements of theory as these; and, as Polanyi has pointed out, much that we learn has to become tacit in this way if we are to apply it fluently in practice. (15) Constantly to have to pause and refer to principles is to be as yet unskilled.

A teacher may also be closer to theory than he thinks through its invisible embodiment in the materials, equipment, buildings and general institutional arrangements which surround him. For example, if he uses certain teaching materials, or is in a building of a certain sort, or is presented with a certain grouping of children, then he will need some knowledge of theory simply fully to be aware of where he is and what he is doing, or alternatively what he has to contend with. Hartnett and Naish claim that any justification of theory must at least show that its results are better than would be obtained simply by starting from scratch. (16) But 'scratch' does not exist in institutionalised education. The whole environment in a school is an artefact, produced in part with the guidance of theoretical conceptions past and present. To set oneself against theory would simply be to make oneself the prisoner of past theories.

Beyond this admixture of theory with practice it might be suggested that teachers would do best to develop their own theories. One can see great advantages in this possibility; the point would be clearly understood, there would be greater personal commitment to carrying the implications into effect, and pragmatic relevance would be assured. But against these great advantages have to be set some serious drawbacks. In the first place, progress is going to be very slow and halting if every individual has, so to speak, to reinvent the wheel. The various theoretical disciplines represent not only an accumulated and constantly refined body of ideas, but also a set of critical tools and standards. Do-it-yourself theory may be effective over a very limited range of problems, but even genius spread over a professional lifetime will not recapitulate the products and standards of a single established discipline.

A more subtle deficiency of do-it-yourself theory is that theory may already be necessary for the most adequate identification of the problem that is the source of the initial practical difficulty. This, of course, is equally a possible deficiency in those who hard-headedly adopt a strict criterion of pragmatic relevance in turning to theory. Consider a man who presents himself in a doctor's surgery as being ill: is his quite clearly a medical problem for which the doctor should now try to find a medical solution? It may be. But equally, and certainly in some cases, the man's problem would be more adequately seen as an ethical one, or a political one, or an occupational one, depending on the root cause.   Analogously, a teacher may identify a troublesome child as presenting a problem in terms of individual perversity.   But it might be more adequate to identify the problem as one of home circumstances, or of inappropriate curricular provision, or of unsuitable school organisation.   Problems are revealed as such within frameworks of understanding, and frequently there are alternative frameworks which may fit better than the obvious or commonsense choice.   Far from its being always best to start from some practical problem and then to look round for, or to generate, a piece of suitable theory, on the contrary we may first need a piece of theory in order to see that there is a problem, or what the problem really is.

It would not be right to close this section on kinds of scepticism as to the desirability of theory for teachers without admitting that the sceptics may, in particular cases, be fully justified.   This is not just because what is offered may be theory of thematic relevance only, when there are urgent practical problems calling for understanding and solution.   It may be that the theory offered is radically misconceived: it may embody spurious science, pretentious humbug, absurd models, or just a wrong turn not yet identified as such.   The debates over the proper nature of the human sciences have their repercussions in educational theory too. (17)   An important part of theorising must therefore be internal criticism. Behavioural conditioning, Piagetian accounts of what young children are said to lack, conceptual analysis in philosophy, the sociology of knowledge: all of these and more have attracted some just criticism.   One of the more reliable inductions in an uncertain world is that error and confusion will continue to be regular features of the theoretical scene.   In this situation comfort may yet be drawn from reflecting that such theorising is not all that there is, and even this usually does have in it at least some element of truth.   Some positive gains can accrue even from a consideration of false theories, such as gains in critical skill.   Small comfort perhaps, but there is no straight or clearly marked road to truth.

IV

I would like finally to consider more closely what is involved in the 'application' of theory to practice.   A presupposition of such application is that there is some distinguishable thing called 'theory' which can then be brought into relation to practice in some way.   At the stage of application the determining influence is from theory to practice, although there may well be influences in the reverse direction at an earlier stage during the formulation and testing of the theory.

Even this very general characterisation already has the
merit of disclosing a possible fraudulent appearance of theory.
There are those, and they would include some who write
prospectuses, who feel that practice is too nakedly unadorned
without some pleasing decorative touches of cosmetic generality.
Still worse is the ideological rationalisation of an existing practice, thus mystifying reality with spurious justifications rather
than providing a deeper understanding of it.   But critics
who tend to see all educational theory in this way ought to be
careful that they do not saw off the very branch they are
themselves sitting on.   For if all theory is said to be fraudulent, then so too will be the higher-order theory in which this
assertion is made.   But I would not wish to deny that there
are real examples of the genre, fully meriting exposure.   The
psychological theories of the Norwood Report might serve as
one example, whereas the suggestion that Hirst's 'forms of
knowledge' theory is simply a rationalisation of the traditional
grammar school curriculum seems to me to be both ill-informed
and unjust.

But to return to the application of genuine theory, we have
to consider both thematic and pragmatic relevance, although
the first only very briefly.   To show application in the
thematic sense, we need only provide some educational illustration of the theoretical conception.   Thus a sociological discussion of 'anticipatory socialisation' might be illustrated,
rather obviously, by reference to the already changing behaviour of someone who is shortly to take up a headship.   A
less obvious example would be to illustrate Sartre's theory of
freedom by reference to teacher labelling activity, or the
effects of fitting children to certain descriptions of them.
The field is wide if thematic relevance is all that we have in
mind.

Pragmatic relevance raises many more difficulties.   In the
first place, this is because a whole mass of considerations, by
no means all or even most of them theoretical, always bears
upon a determinate practical judgement.   For example, if the
policy is considered of integrating the curriculum, such untheoretical questions will immediately arise as whether the
school can afford any new materials that may be needed, how
Smith will react to the change, and what the time-table implications will be.   But an equally pertinent set of theoretical
questions may be asked, such as what is being assumed about
the nature of knowledge, what the effect is likely to be on
professional identities and teacher hierarchies, and whether
historical or foreign examples can be found which offer sug-
gestive comparisons.   No doubt the ideal of comprehensiveness towards which these questions tend can never be realised,
but a cut-off point cannot be chosen without arbitrariness.

In respect of the great variety of considerations which have
to be borne in mind, although not of course in every other
respect, practical judgement in teaching is rather like practical
judgement in engineering.   The designer of a machine has to
combine theoretical considerations to do with materials, stress
and fatigue with many other considerations, such as those of
safety, ease of maintenance, whether standard parts can be
incorporated, what the operator's point of view is likely to be,
the competitiveness of final market price, and so on.   In both
cases theory alone would very likely fail to anticipate the rich-
ness of practical experience.   The lecturer who, guided by
Piagetian theories, outlines a practical lesson on rigid and
flexible shapes may well fail to foresee that a careful child
putting together a supposedly 'flexible' shape may produce
something much more rigid than a fumbler who botches the
making of a supposedly 'rigid' one.   Rather similarly, the
language of maintenance men becomes especially colourful when
they are confronted with having to adjust an inaccessible
mechanism that has been made so because theory indicated that
it would need no adjustments.   Marxist criticisms of the division of intellectual from manual labour turn in part on misfor-
tunes such as these.

The notion of pragmatically relevant application is further
complicated in a way not quite paralleled in engineering.   The
application of educational theory is mediated by the teacher's
personality in a much more intimate way than in engineering
design, since his temperament, values and abilities may importantly condition the application of a particular piece of theory.
Differences in final practical judgement, sometimes quite legitimate differences, may thus be attributable to personality differences: in tolerance of noise, or in ability to divide attention, or in the weight attached to conflicting principles, for
example.

The great variety of the considerations which legitimately
bear upon practice, only some of them theoretical, explains
how a project may be theoretically possible but in practice not
possible.   In theory, there may be nothing against and even
everything to be said for the reduction of class sizes to a
maximum of ten, but some quite untheoretical and straightforwardly financial considerations may well mean that this measure
is practically impossible.   However, theoretical considerations
may alone be decisive where their bearing is negative.   If
something is theoretically impossible, then it must be impossible
in practice too.   For instance, if theory correctly indicates
certain physiological, or psychological, or conceptual conditions
to be necessary for practical success, then the absence of
these conditions, quite apart from any other considerations,
will doom the project to failure.   But it will not necessarily
follow, of course, that we can only sit around and wait for

more auspicious circumstances to arise of themselves.   Readiness can sometimes be actively brought about.

Yet a further complication for pragmatic relevance is that
every consideration derived from theory retains a certain
generality.   For example, you could not determine purely on
theoretical grounds at just what age to end compulsory schooling, which may well explain the theoretical poverty of yesterday's debate over raising the school-leaving age from 15 to 16.
Again, general principles do not apply themselves, and the
final particular application of a piece of theory therefore requires an unteachable act of judgement.   Because of this, a
relevant application of theory may be missed.   A teacher may
have followed and participated in a theoretical discussion of
whether there are general powers of the mind, such as problem-solving skill or imagination.   But on some subsequent
occasion he may list a general capacity to be 'observant' as a
category of assessment on a proposed record card, without
any recognition of the possible application of those discussions
to this particular case.

Immanuel Kant saw very clearly that particular judgements
have to be made by ourselves when he wrote:

And it thus appears that, though understanding is capable of
being instructed, and of being equipped with rules, judgement is a peculiar talent which can be practised only, and
cannot be taught.   It is the specific quality of so-called
mother-wit;   and its lack no school can make good. (18)

Part of Kant's argument for saying that was that if you try
to overcome this difficulty by providing rules for judgement,
these rules will in turn require further rule-escaping acts of
judgement for their application.   In this area can perhaps be
found at least the germinal basis for a claim that teaching requires a capacity for professional judgement.   But by the
same token, it must be admitted that theory can never lead
the teacher right up to final particular practical applications.

Towards the final stages of particularising theoretical considerations, many other things can go wrong.   The theoretical
conception may of course itself be flawed right from the start,
as some of them certainly are.   A recent investigation found
an infant school guided by a theoretical conception in terms of
which the teachers could have approached 'success' only by
producing a totally unmanageable situation. (19)   Again, it
can happen that the theory is all right, but the teacher is
self-deceived in thinking that he is implementing it.   He may
think that he is guided by certain egalitarian conceptions,
when in fact he is giving far more attention to the assertive;
and sometimes sound intentions are of course blocked by external constraints.

Much of what I have said about 'application' has concerned
existing practices and the bearing of theory on these by way
of illuminating or modifying commentary.   A final difficulty
worth mentioning relates more to the bearing of theory on the
devising of new or alternative practices.   Here it must be
said that such novelties cannot be derived from theory, as it
were by deduction, but require a power of creative synthesis.
Granted everything in the way of theory and much else, still
an efficient, economical and temporally ordered sequence of
actions has to be envisaged.   An original response from the
side of practice is needed: a suggested institutional arrange-
ment, a teaching technique, a way of organising materials, a
new practical aid, or a way of handling certain situations.
It is not a lamentable deficiency of theory that such a creative
synthesis lies beyond it, since the matter could not be otherwise.   But the gap does cause many difficulties in securing
the fruitful interaction of theory and practice.

Such considerations as these have led some people to make
change in behaviour the acid test of the relevance of theory.
It is then asked what the teacher will do differently as a
result of learning some theory.   But this demand could be in
several ways unfair.   In some circumstances, not to change
in the face of certain pressures may be precisely the benefit
gained from acquaintance with theory.   Faced with pressure
to introduce some new but ephemeral curricular fashion, it
may be a theoretically informed conception which rightly and
successfully leads the resistance to this.   Then again, theory
may produce beneficial changes without being tied to any specific change in behaviour, for example changes in attitude,
perspective, commitment, or the sense of intellectual challenge
in one's work.   If a managerial stance is implicit in the re-
quest for specific behavioural change, as it often is, then it
deserves noticing that someone other than the teacher is here
assuming the right to specify in what particular direction the
teacher's behaviour should change.   This is at variance with
a common understanding of what is implied by the teacher's
professional judgement.   For that reason, a bid to assert a
tighter control over teachers, and to make them into function-
aries with narrowly defined duties, would probably seek, as a
first step, to deny them access to theoretical discussion.

Yet it does not seem unreasonable to expect the application
of theory to make *some* difference, even if it is too narrowly
restrictive to insist on the prediction of specific behavioural
changes.   For example, it would not be easy to see what the
possible pragmatic relevance could be of management studies
for teaching in a non-institutional setting, as with the informal
groups arranged under the auspices of 'Education Otherwise'. (20)   Presumably large tracts of sociology would have
little relevance for teachers of highly selected and like-minded

groups such as may still sometimes constitute a university
tutorial or seminar.   But the typical school situation is not
like this.   It involves learners who vary greatly in ability,
outlook, age, attitude, background and behaviour; it involves
great complexities of both curriculum and of organisation; and
it calls for the initiation or assimilation of continual change.
Faced with all this, the only reasonable questions to theory
would seem to be what kind, how much, in what way, for
whom, where and when, but not whether at all.

What changes, then, may reasonably be expected from the
application of theory to practice in education?   Different
branches of theory will have different strengths and weaknesses here, depending for example on the level at which decisions are being made, but it is a reasonable hope that there
will be gains in respect of at least some of the following: (1)
a deeper grasp of the nature of learning, and of the implications of various teaching strategies; (2) a more adequate and
considered set of educational values, with an appreciation of
their curricular and methodological implications; (3) a deeper
understanding of the background or context which provides
the setting for educational practice; (4) a certain imaginative
liberation through seeing the actual distanced, and thus revealed as only one possibility; (5) and, quite generally, a
degree of reconstruction of ideas through a critical reconsideration of their truth and adequacy, and hence greater intellectual control over practice.

Such changes as these are the objects of a reasonable hope,
but they cannot be transformed into specific behavioural pre-
dictions.   Lest the hard-headed should still feel dissatisfied
with this result, let me recall some of the reasons why it must
be so.   Even granted that we have some genuine piece of
theory that is pragmatically relevant, still these theoretical
beliefs have to take their place in a complex ecology of other
beliefs, some of which will even be beyond recall.   The
theoretical are only one of many sets of considerations which
properly bear upon a final particular practical judgement.
For instance, to know something of the history of the education of women, to be aware of the processes of sex-typing, or
to be sensitive to different kinds of possible discrimination
and their usual justification, all have a bearing on the practical decision whether girls should do metalwork, but these
theoretical considerations cannot by themselves fully determine
an answer to that question.   If a general rule or principle
should be arrived at, an unteachable act of judgement would
still be needed in giving it final application to situations which
will always be in some degree unpredictable.   Finally, the
necessary mediation through the teacher's own individual personality may quite properly introduce a further variable which
precludes standard solutions.

V

It has been said, not of educational but of metaphysical theories, that they are like fortresses which are subjected to constant attack, never actually taken, then one day it is realised
that there is no-one inside any more.   But much as some
self-styled practical men may wish it, it is very unlikely that
such a desertion will be the fate of educational theory.   What
kind of theory has most to offer to educational practice may be
a real question, but whether theory can have anything at all
to offer is not.

Nevertheless, both theorising and the teaching of theory are
beset with difficulties, many of which still remain even if the
nature of theory and its relations to practice are satisfactorily
clarified.   In the teaching of theory, as with teaching of
every kind, the practices adopted are always unstable compro-
mises between conflicting considerations.   Theorising itself
contains such finally unresolvable tensions as those between
doing justice to the standards set by pure disciplines and
being governed by criteria of pragmatic relevance, or between
the advantages of a specialised division of labour and the
danger of getting out of touch, or between the passion to
understand a matter fully before deciding and the peremptory
needs of action now.   More prosaically, we may say that the
educational theorist is inherently subject to severe role conflict.   But he should not feel embattled as well.   It is not
so much that he should retreat into a fort and see that it is
defended, as that defence should not be more than an occa-
sional need at all.

REFERENCES

1 See, for example, Peters, R.S. (1965), 'Education as Initiation' (London, Evans Brothers), p. 7.
2 O'Connor, D.J. (1957), 'The Philosophy of Education'
   (London, Routledge & Kegan Paul), p. 110.
3 Wilson, J. (1975), 'Educational Theory and the Preparation
   of Teachers' (Windsor, NFER).
4 Hartnett, A. and Naish, M. (eds) (1976), 'Theory and the
   Practice of Education', 2 volumes (London, Heinemann).
5 Tibble, J. (ed.) (1966), 'The Study of Education' (London,
   Routledge & Kegan Paul), ch. 3.
6 Ibid., p. 126.
7 Ibid., p. 210.
8 See Langford, G. and O'Connor, D.J. (eds) (1973), 'New
   Essays in Philosophy of Education' (London, Routledge &
   Kegan Paul), chs 3 and 4.
9 See Perry, L.R. (1966), Objective and practical history,
   'Proceedings of the Philosophy of Education Society', 1,
   pp. 35-48.

10 Naish, M. and Hartnett, A. (1975), What theory cannot do
    for teachers, 'Education for Teaching', no. 98, pp. 12-19.
11 Ryle, G. (1949), 'The Concept of Mind' (London, Hutchin-
    son), ch. 2.
12 E.g. Lloyd, D.I. (1976), Theory and practice, 'Proceed-
    ings of the Philosophy of Education Society', 10, p. 102.
13 See for example, Moore, T. (1974), 'Educational Theory'
    (London, Routledge & Kegan Paul), p. 97.
14 As in Dewey, J. (1963 edn), 'Experience and Education'
    (London, Collier-Macmillan), ch. 2.
15 Polanyi, M. (1967), 'The Tacit Dimension' (London, Rout-
    ledge & Kegan Paul).
16 Naish, M. and Hartnett, A. (1975), ibid., p. 18.
17 See, for example, Oakeshott, M. (1975), On the theoreti-
    cal understanding of human conduct, in his 'On Human
    Conduct' (Oxford, Clarendon).
18 Kant, I. (1781), 'Critique of Pure Reason', B172.
19 Sharp, R. and Green, A. (1975), 'Education and Social
    Control' (London, Routledge & Kegan Paul), ch. 6.
20 The reference is to a group of parents who take their title
    from the 1944 Education Act, para. 36 (... either by regu-
    lar attendance at school or otherwise).

2 PHILOSOPHY OF EDUCATION 1952-1982

I

Throughout the 1950s, and in direct response to developments in general philosophy, a new conception of philosophy of education was slowly forming and finding sporadic expression. But all of this was very far from a state of affairs in which it would become natural to think of educational studies as divided into various disciplines, of which philosophy of education would be one. Yet by 1977, Mary Warnock could uncontroversially open her book 'Schools of Thought' by saying that 'it cannot any longer be seriously doubted that there is such a thing as the philosophy of education'. How did this transition come about?

The opportunity came in the early 1960s. The teacher training colleges were extending their certificate courses from two to three years, while the Robbins Report was recommending that the colleges themselves be redesignated 'colleges of education' and that, for some students, there should be a new education degree, the BEd. These changes combined to require more and academically better qualified lecturers and new courses which would be of a rigour deserving the award of a degree.

A comparable change was taking place in the USA where such bitter critics of the 'Mickey Mouse' education courses offered to teachers as J.B. Conant and J.D. Koerner were urging a much stronger grounding in the disciplines relevant to education. Yet a further factor in the creation of an opportunity for new academic initiatives was the state of the schools, in which many controversial changes were taking place, such as the 'revolution' in the primary schools, reorganisation at the secondary level and the trial runs of various curriculum development projects. There was never a time more ripe for someone to mark out the claims of any newly emerging discipline of education.

So far as philosophy of education was concerned, the opportunity was taken, and with maximum impact, by Reid's successor at London, Professor R.S. Peters. Peters's background in general philosophy, coupled with a long-standing interest in education, fired him with a missionary zeal to raise the stan-

dards of educational theorising.   His inaugural lecture, given
in 1963 with the title 'Education as Initiation', was published
in the following year as a booklet of forty-two pages. (1)   It
intimated an agenda of topics for discussion and gave a paradigm of method which were formative for the decade to follow.
Topics woven into his theme included the debate between trad-
itionalists and progressives, the education of the emotions, the
nature of creativity and of critical thinking, the role of the eco-
nomist's and the sociologist's views of education and the relations of means to ends in education.   Various points were
linked with the historical views of Plato, Quintilian, Froebel,
Dewey and Whitehead.

But the centrepiece, and it was this that was taken as the
paradigm of method, was the analysis of the concept of education.   Peters argued, as has by now become very familiar,
that 'education' is a family of morally legitimate procedures
which aim to develop intrinsically worthwhile states of mind
with wide-ranging cognitive content.   The process as a whole
was conceived by Peters as a development of mind through initiation into public traditions which incorporate impersonal standards and which, if mastered, give a distinctive quality to
life.   Peters's fuller statement of his views, which also
brought in his strong interest in ethics and social philosophy
to add to his already apparent interest in philosophy of mind,
appeared in his book 'Ethics and Education' (1966).

In his inaugural, Peters had characterised philosophical
concerns as being to do with the demarcation of concepts and
the grounds of knowledge.   In fact this second, epistemological aspect was developed in Britain more by Paul Hirst, who
was also in the London department at that time, though from
America Israel Scheffler's 'Conditions of Knowledge' (1965)
came to be widely used.   Peters did probe the grounds of
certain knowledge claims, especially in ethics in terms of the
'transcendental deduction', but it was Hirst who was to make
the greater impact in terms of general epistemology.

Hirst's article Liberal Education and the Nature of Knowledge
soon became a classic. (2)   Not just fellow philosophers of
education but also members of the Inspectorate, writers of
Schools Council working papers as well as students and
teachers became aware of the 'forms of knowledge' and pon-
dered their implications for curriculum and method.   This
thesis readily combined with Peters's more formal account of
education to provide a powerful synthesis, expressed in Hirst
and Peters's jointly authored book 'The Logic of Education'
(1970).   This synthesis found no equally well articulated
rival, though some might have seen Phenix's 'Realms of Meaning' (1964) as such.

Hirst had already in 1963 written another article which also rapidly gained the status of a classic.   This was his Philosophy and Educational Theory. (3)   Here he argued that there was no single discipline of education and that philosophy was itself but one of several disciplines each having their distinctive bearing on educational principles and practice.   A revised version of this article stated the argument for an approach through the disciplines in J.W. Tibble's 'The Study of Education' (1966), which also served as the lead publication for a whole new publishing venture of Routledge & Kegan Paul's: the Student's Library of Education series.   While Hirst was thus locating the contribution of philosophy, Peters was providing a manifesto on its nature and content for the colleges, in his paper The Place of Philosophy in the Training of Teachers. (4)

There followed a burst of activity which scarcely seems credible in the sober, not to say sombre, 1980s.   Courses in philosophy of education at all levels and in all teacher education institutions (save the Open University) were offered and were even mandatory.   Many new specialist appointments had to be made to cope with the demand.   Philosophers began to occupy chairs in education in addition to Peters's own at the London Institute, first Perry and Hirst, and rather later Elliott, Dearden, Sockett, Pring and Aspin.   Pure philosophers, such as Professors Hamlyn, Hare, Oakeshott, O'Connor, Passmore, D.Z. Phillips, A. Phillips Griffiths and Ryle also took an interest, which was greatly facilitated by Peters's established reputation amongst general philosophers.   In 1973, the Royal Institute of Philosophy combined with the by then existing Philosophy of Education Society to hold a major conference at the University of Exeter, the proceedings of which eventually appeared in book form as 'Philosophers Discuss Education' (1975), edited by Stuart Brown.

There was also a publications explosion.   Peters himself added the International Library of the Philosophy of Education to the philosophical branch of Routledge's Student's Library of Education series.   Influential collections appeared, such as T.H. Hollins's 'Aims in Education' (1964), R.D. Archambault's 'Philosophical Analysis and Education' (1965), Peters's 'The Concept of Education' (1967) and Dearden, Hirst and Peters's 'Education and the Development of Reason' (1972).   Peters also edited a collection for the Oxford Readings in Philosophy series under the title 'Philosophy of Education' (1973), while Hirst collected together many of his articles in his 'Knowledge and the Curriculum' (1974).   My own 'Philosophy of Primary Education' (1968) gave a more specific focus to some general themes and was widely used in the colleges.   John Wilson and Robin Barrow both wrote extensively.   Nor did all publishing originate in the universities.   Particularly strong philosophy

of education departments at Stockwell and Homerton Colleges
produced such collections as D.I. Lloyd's 'Philosophy and the
Teacher' (1976) and Bridges and Scrimshaw's 'Values and
Authority in Schools' (1976).

Since 1941 there had been a Philosophy of Education Society
in the USA but towards the end of 1965 Peters set about
founding a Philosophy of Education Society of Great Britain.
Its first annual general meeting and the publication of its first
set of proceedings took place in 1966.   Peters was himself
chairman, while Louis Arnaud Reid was asked to be the first
president and Hirst brought formative influence to bear as the
first secretary.   Since 1978 the proceedings have been re-
titled the 'Journal of Philosophy of Education' to make clear
that the publication is not confined to the proceedings of the
annual conference.   The journal now appears in two issues a
year and by the end of 1980 altogether 169 articles had
appeared by 113 different authors, and the journal was being
taken in forty-four different countries.   Membership of the
society was between 400 and 500 and as well as the regular
national meetings in London, meetings were also being held in
some fourteen branches round the country.

II

The 'revolution' in philosophy of education which took place in
the 1960s, not only in Britain but also in North America and
Australasia, involved greater consciousness of an involvement
with the methods and results of philosophy as an academic
discipline.   These methods and results were directly applied
to educational questions (which presupposed rather more of an
acquaintance with the parent discipline than some lecturers
possessed, or could readily acquire in the rapid expansion of
opportunities).   Most importantly of all, this influence by the
parent discipline carried with it the then fashionable paradigm,
which was that of linguistic philosophy.

Linguistic philosophy looked to 'ordinary use' as its guide.
Different senses of some ordinary term, or neighbouring terms,
would be distinguished.   Points would be substantiated by
reference to 'what we would say', 'what we would call' and
'what would count as'.   Linguistic intuitions would be explored
to see what some term 'suggested' or what it 'sounds odd to
say'.   Strictly, the object of the inquiry was not the English
word but the concept which it marked out.   Such concepts
might be the same across different languages, or might not be
handily marked out by a single word at all.   Concepts also
needed to be distinguished from the more or less personal psychological associations which a word might have for some individual.   If things went well, then criteria for the application

of the concept would hopefully be laid out, amounting in
especially favourable cases to a set of necessary and sufficient
conditions.   If the going was less easy, then one might have
to identify the 'central' uses, setting aside as secondary those
cases that could not so easily be fitted under the concept.

The origins of this style of philosophising were found as far
back as Socrates and Aristotle, though the more immediate
stimulus to it came, in different ways, from Wittgenstein and
J.L. Austin.   Philosophy was conceived as a fight against
bewitchment by language, best waged by looking at 'language
games' and their associated 'forms of life'.   Ordinary language
was regarded by Austin as a repository of subtle distinctions
which had been forged, tried and tested in everyday life and
which were likely to be more sound than any rationalistic pre-
scriptions of disengaged philosophers.

This relation to 'life' was important because, without it,
references to linguistic habits and intuitions would have
seemed so incredibly flimsy as a basis for anything as not to
deserve taking seriously.   Nevertheless, there was a paradox
in the whole approach, namely that in ordinary language 'philosophy' is *not* some kind of study of ordinary language.
Disconcerting also was the practice of making 'conceptual
points' by means of deliberately trivial examples.   This was
done for the understandable reason of not wishing to get
bogged down in controversy over a fairly arbitrary choice of
example, so losing sight of the main point.   But it was disconcerting to find grand themes of ethics apparently degener-
ating into criteria for the grading of apples, or even for
assessing sewage effluent.

Peters's paradigmatic example of the analysis of education
was in a linguistic style, with appropriate references to what
we would say, what the term suggests, what the dictionary
records, and so on.   In reality, Peters always did very much
more than this programme would require.   He brought in his
considerable knowledge of psychology, his experience of a
variety of educational institutions and his extensive knowledge
of the history of philosophy.   Far from just recording 'uses',
he articulated a comprehensive ethical and social philosophical
position and extensively worked out its educational implications.   But the stated paradigm stuck, later reinforced by a
further paradigmatic analysis of 'punishment'.   An early sign
that all might not be well with this approach was a persistent
tendency for students to decline to recognise 'ordinary use' in
what was put to them, but to refer instead to 'the philosophical sense', while disputes over the correct analysis of 'education' were endless.

Serious doubts about linguistic analysis were already spread-

ing in the parent discipline, while thoughtful and constructive
critics like Abraham Edel, (5) and hostile sociological ones
like David Adelstein, (6) were raising fundamental difficulties
specifically related to Peters's own work. The broadly
Marxist mood of the period of student unrest in the late
1960s, and the horrors of the Vietnam War, were making
value-neutrality, which was a supposed virtue of linguistic
analysis, seem irresponsible. If philosophers could find
nothing better to do than, so to speak, cock an ear for linguistic nuances, then they were likely to be ignored, as well
as to be pilloried by Ernest Gellner. (7)   Linguistic philosophy created the impression that philosophy was a trivial
squabble over words, or a perverse focusing of attention just
on the finger of someone intent on pointing at a reality.

Was philosophy really just a linguistic technique?   Did its
subject matter have no history, or at least require no knowledge of that history for an understanding of it?   Might not
'ordinary use' be confused or inconsistent?   What would be
the 'ordinary use' for some quite new term?   When was an
analysis 'correct'?   If philosophers are really describing ordinary use, ought they not to be out doing some sort of empirical survey work?   If analysis 'leaves everything as it is',
what is the point of it?   And if it is said that the point of
analysis is to clear our heads so as to reveal 'further questions', whose job is it to answer those, especially as they may
well seem to be the really important questions?   Again, could
use and meaning really be equated, for one might very well
know the use of a word such as 'amen' but not know its
meaning.

To my mind, however, two major criticisms stand out.   The
first arises from taking much more seriously the already ack-
nowledged connections between concepts and 'life'.   Concepts
reflect interests, frequently competing interests, especially in
a practical field such as education.   It is not that the Latin
'educare' is struggling with the Latin 'educere' in some ether-
eal medium but that people and groups are contending for different things.   As Marxist critics were quick to point out,
the linguistic philosopher's 'we' may therefore be a disguised
sectional interest bidding for universal validity.

Again, when teachers say they 'teach children and not subjects', is it really just that they have failed to grasp a point
of grammar?   To offer the prospect of major benefit, linguistic analysis must assume that conflicts are due to the conceptual confusion which it unravels, and that its concepts actually
apply to reality.   Neither of these two assumptions may be
justified.   Edel supplied an interesting example of how a
wider perspective might be taken when he related the distinction between 'knowing that' and 'knowing how' to the division

of mental and manual labour in society and the differing traditions of liberal and vocational education. (8)

The second criticism follows on from the first, and concerns
the supposed value-neutrality of linguistic analysis.   Why has
this concept been chosen for analysis?   Is there not some
version of the naturalistic fallacy committed in passing from a
description of use to a judgement that it is correct use?   Will
the historic act of analysing not itself be a help, a hindrance
or a distraction to some cause?   May not analysis very well
embody a species of conservatism, serving to give ideological
reassurance to those resisting change?   Is analysis confined
to picking old bones when the battle is over, like Hegel's Owl
of Minerva?

It remains true that philosophers nevertheless do well to be
sensitive to language.   It is not pedantry accurately to determine the meaning of what is said, or the sense in which it is
meant, for that is a necessary preliminary to the appraisal of
its truth.   Without clear propositions and dependency relations, validity and truth cannot be assessed.   And many
useful preliminary distinctions were marked out and remain
from the linguistic period: between education and training,
between being in and being an authority, between being interested in and being in one's interests, between being neutral in
intention and neutral in effect, between teaching that, how to
and to, between needs and wants, and so on.

The strongest recent reaffirmation of a linguistic approach to
conceptual analysis has come from John Wilson, from whose
prolific pen one might choose as a major example his book
'Preface to the Philosophy of Education' (1979) or his article
Concepts, Contestability and the Philosophy of Education. (9)
But even he places this analysis in a wider context by seeking
to show certain concepts not to be optional, and by construing
analysis as being at the same time a kind of psychotherapy.

III

Concerning possible alternatives, one might have expected a
distinctive Catholic school of philosophy of education to have
developed, but this has not happened.   Many philosophers of
education are Catholics but they generally follow the main-
stream in their choice of topics and methods.   The nearest to
a distinctive Catholic perspective is probably Jacques Maritain's
book 'Education at the Crossroads' (1943), though this has had
very little influence.

Pure philosophers continue to take a lively and invigorating
interest in philosophy of education and a steady stream of

books appears from that direction.   For example, Downie, Loudfoot and Telfer have written on 'Education and Personal Relationships' (1974), and Antony Flew criticised the 'new sociology of education' in 'Sociology, Equality and Education' (1976).   Mary Warnock presented a new view of aims in her 'Schools of Thought' (1977), while David Hamlyn ranged over the work of Piaget and Chomsky in his 'Knowledge and the Growth of Understanding' (1978).   Most recently, David Cooper has examined egalitarianism in his 'Illusions of Equality' (1980), R.F. Holland has written 'Against Empiricism' (1980), John Passmore has discussed 'The Philosophy of Teaching' (1980) and Anthony O'Hear has written a new introduction to philosophy of education called 'Education, Society and Human Nature' (1981).

Phenomenology represents another possible approach, but Curtis and Mays's 'Phenomenology and Education' (1978), which was an edited collection of conference papers, appears to have convinced no one that here was a fruitful new approach.   In a review article on the book, one of the most scholarly contemporary phenomenologists in education, Francis Dunlop, argued that many of the contributors are not even very clear what phenomenology is.   Dunlop himself takes the work of Husserl as the essential point of origin for the movement. Phenomenological arguments, however, are apt to have much the same character as ethical intuitionism in containing more assertion than argument.

Much of R.K. Elliott's work might be regarded as phenomenological, yet by contrast it explores what introspection and subjective experience might have to yield in a way that is of very much more than private interest.   Elliott's major articles on Education and Human Being (10) and Education and Justification (11) were a powerful critique of certain theses in Hirst and Peters, though they did not amount to a fully developed alternative conception.   Elliott's articles on aesthetics and the imagination have also been greatly valued. (12)

Marxist criticisms of philosophy of education have stemmed largely from writers in the social sciences, such as Michael Young, Madan Sarup and Bowles and Gintis, but in 'Education and Knowledge' (1979) Kevin Harris proposed a materialist paradigm for future philosophical work and clearly saw his book as a new start in the philosophy of education.   Marxist analyses seem generally to turn on two major claims.   The first claim is that the ways in which we conceive of reality are socially constructed, and in a qualified sense this is probably true.   The second claim is that a ruling class exploits the rest, especially through the medium of educational institutions, by a 'structured misrepresentation of reality'.

The method of analysis is then to 'lay bare' where this exploitation is occurring.   Educational arrangements are 'demystified' in a way which exhibits pupils and teachers alike as being conned into serving not their own interests but those of the ruling class.   The learner, like the factory worker, is seen as alienated and indeed the alienation of the first is seen as being preparation for the alienation of the second.   Some writers, such as Esland, are massively and depressingly cynical.   Nothing is what it seems for them: if you try to say something true, you are really bolstering your power by defining reality; if you try to discover the truth, you are really negotiating it; if you try to justify anything, you are engaging in the rhetoric of legitimation.   An air of scandalous revelation pervades it all, though like much scandal it is rarely substantiated, the arguments of Bowles and Gintis being exceptional in this respect.

It would appear that Marxist analyses may so bewitch their authors and their audiences with the sense of being privy to a final unveiling of the real truth that they lose a robust sense of reality.   'Truth and objectivity are human products' Gorbutt asserts, characteristically not noticing what this would imply for the status of his own assertions. (13)   But whether we are discovering a pre-existing reality or creating a new one, there are limits to the concepts that will be found to have, or that can be given, application, not to mention requirements of consistency.   In the vogue for finding fraudulent ideology everywhere, more attention could profitably be given to the severe conditions that any such ideology must meet if it is to be remotely plausible.   The revelation of ideology and alienation (and there surely is some to reveal) is itself of presumptive interest only because there are universal values, such as truth, justice, liberty and self-realisation. These values are evident in more constructive, less cynical work such as Harold Entwistle's 'Class, Culture and Education' (1978) or in his commentary 'Antonio Gramsci' (1979).

There are, however, two broad redirections of attention for which Marxist critics have been at least partly responsible and with some benefit.   The first of these is towards the connections between education and work, or the backwash from the division of labour in society.   The ways in which schooling is functional or non-functional in this respect, and whether it is so intentionally or unintentionally, certainly deserve attention, both empirical and philosophical.   The second is towards a much livelier sense of what seems natural, or is taken for granted, as really being chosen, whether deliberately or by default.   This is, of course, also a strong theme in the existentialism of such philosophers as Heidegger and Sartre, the common root being the idealist element of meaning-bestowal and spontaneity.   The excesses to which these insights have nevertheless led are well exposed in the later chapters of David Cooper's 'Illusions of Equality' (1980), though Richard Pring's aptly titled article Knowledge out of Control (14) and his book 'Knowledge and Schooling' (1976) were an earlier, much needed exposure of some serious epistemological shortcomings in the genre.

IV

If linguistic, phenomenological and Marxist modes of argument are each limited in their usefulness, as I claim that they are, what paradigm might serve better?   Should philosophers of education perhaps return to their historical predecessors? Although the 'history of educational ideas' tended to be swept aside in the self-confident optimism of the 1960s, earlier philosophers have never been quite lost from view.   Robin Barrow in his 'Plato, Utilitarianism and Education' (1975) re-examined the writings of Plato.   John White, in an interesting joint authorship with a historian, has looked at the idealist tradition of educational reformers in 'Philosophers as Educational Reformers' (1979).   F.W. Garforth at Hull has produced several books on different historical philosophers and Peters's book 'Essays on Educators' (1981) similarly looks back.   Much benefit can still be gained from Dewey's classic 'Democracy and Education' (1916) for its comprehensiveness, its historical sense and its awareness of other disciplines.   But Dewey's arguments lack sharpness, he was elusive on fundamental questions of value and he overdid the role of science as a model for all problem-solving.   Dewey was reassessed in Peters's collection 'John Dewey Re-considered' (1977).

I do not myself think that philosophy of education stands in any need of a single paradigm.   Its patterns and strategies of argument should be tailored to the subject matter under discussion, which is normally certain general concepts, principles, positions or practices.   It should make any necessary distinctions to clarify meaning, explore conceptual possibilities and try to identify what is necessary and what is contingent. It should expose question-begging, misleading claims and inconsistency.   It should draw implications, show the full extent of someone's commitments, reveal absurd consequences, highlight by parallel arguments, draw attention to unnoticed alternatives and test assumptions.   It should probe the validity of justifications, draw attention to areas of undeserved neglect, redress serious imbalances and assemble pertinent reminders.

Further, philosophy of education should expose narrow conceptions, probe presuppositions and reveal hidden connections, or expose spurious unity.   It should clarify ideals and

articulate imaginative new conceptions.   It should redescribe
to bring into different focus, show how certain notions will or
will not do the work expected of them, show how one thing
prevents the recognition of another, identify misplaced emphases or misdirected attention and set things in a wider illuminating context.   All of this and more carries us far beyond
the narrowness of a linguistic technique, indifferent even as
to its subject matter.   It is a mode of critical thinking related to an evolving tradition of inquiry which it would be doc-
trinal to try to render more precise.

Amongst the many values implicit in these activities should
be consistency, truth and adequacy.   By 'adequacy' I mean
doing justice to the question and the issues which it raises.
This will typically imply an awareness of the range of interests with which the question is tangled, something of the historical context and the possible further implications.   In fact
even in the linguistic period much work of this broader kind
was done.   When Peters, in his inaugural lecture, used a
linguistic paradigm to examine education, and contrasted his
own approach with the more synthetic approach of his pre-
decessor, he did less than justice to the contributions which
he then himself proceeded to make.   For his work on the
education of the emotions, motivation, moral education, behaviourism, the transcendental deduction and various social principles itself amounted to an ambitious synthesis.   The wide
range of Peters's output can be seen in his collections of his
own papers 'Psychology and Ethical Development' (1974) and
'Education and the Education of Teachers' (1977).

To illustrate the generality of theme and the variety of critical tactics which are characteristic of philosophy of education,
I will very briefly outline some issues which have been of continuing interest.   As a first example, I take Hirst's still
very influential 'forms of knowledge' thesis.   This was to the
effect that propositional knowledge is of some seven or so
irreducibly different kinds, each having their own distinctive
categorial concepts and truth-tests.   The thesis had the
widest of educational implications as is evident from the echoes
of it that are to be found in many working papers, official
reports and articles.   It was a bold conception, providing a
coherent modern version of what a liberal education might be.
It had implications for the possibility of curricular integration,
balance, mental abilities and development, and the nature of
the teacher's authority.

The thesis has, however, not been short of critics, quite
apart from certain sociologists whose philosophical naivety
promptly led them into a crude misunderstanding of it.   The
very notion of a 'form' has been declared unclear.   The list
of the forms has been challenged in its completeness and

indeed its correctness.   Is religion really a form of *know-ledge*?   Does history have distinctive concepts?   Is not geo-metry a very different 'form' from algebra?   The conception of a distinctive truth-test has been argued to be much too simple and the analytic strategy has been seen as scientistic. The exhaustiveness of the division has been challenged on the grounds that much commonsense knowledge appears to fall into none of the forms, so that it must be a set of specialised disciplines which are being described.   In that case, the forms will not be the conditions of any possible experience or of all mental development.   If that is true, will the forms not then lack universality and be historically relative?   And what of justification?   Why attach importance to an initiation into forms of knowledge?   Surely their importance cannot lie just in their formal distinctiveness?   And can they really be re-garded as being of equal weight?

This cannot be the place to assess the validity of each of these criticisms, or such alternative conceptions as Elliott's. At least two important elements of the original thesis seem to come through as of lasting interest: that knowledge is not all of a piece and that this diversity could well have a bearing on ideas of balance in the curriculum.   And since Hirst's thesis will not be in every way totally different from any other, then many of the insights generated in this debate will have much wider applications.

A second continuing theme with wide implications is that of behaviourism.   By this I mean the Skinnerian thesis that 'mental life and the world in which it is lived are inven-tions', (15) the preferred alternative conception being that of an organism emitting incipient movements which can be shaped into desired topographies by controlling the environmental contingencies of reinforcement.   Philosophers of education have, for a change, been at one with Marxists in attacking this doctrine, though on somewhat different grounds.

A first difficulty has been to understand the unit of 'behav-iour', since physical movements are highly ambiguous in their meaning.   It has been argued that human behaviour is not to be understood without reference to the person's beliefs, desires, intentions and self-images, which link more widely still with a social world of customs, practices, rules and insti-tutions.   Apart from this web of shared understanding, we have no criterion for what the unit of behaviour is supposed to be.   There are still further problems of how, apart from such an understanding, appropriate reinforcers can be chosen and how they are to be connected with what they are supposed to reinforce.   And how does the Skinnerian propose to get the 'first instance' of a line of behaviour he wishes to shape in, say, learning physics or French, or appreciating poetry?

Whereas the arguments surrounding Hirst's thesis are concerned to test the validity of a positive conception, those surrounding Skinnerian behaviourism are designed more to avert
an educational disaster.   For behaviourism is likely, as Hugh
Sockett argued in his book 'Designing the Curriculum' (1976),
to narrow educational objectives, to confine what is taught to
what can be measured and to produce 'teaching for the test'.
So far is it from being an ethically neutral technology that it
typically presupposes that experimental 'subjects' must be
adapted to unchanged institutions, and it incorporates a very
limited version of utilitarianism as its ethic.   It may even
take on a note of messianism.   In so far as the practices of
'behaviour modification' escape these dangers, it is probably
because the practitioners are more human than their doctrine
and are really only making more systematic and intelligent use
of ordinary encouragement and discouragement.

As a final example of a philosophical topic that has been of
continuing interest, we might take personal autonomy considered as an educational aim.   Whereas at first this was discussed chiefly in the context of moral education, it was soon
realised that this was a value relevant to the whole curriculum.
I traced its connections with progressivism in my book 'The
Philosophy of Primary Education' (1964) and with discovery
methods in 'Problems in Primary Education' (1976), while J.P.
White, in his book 'Towards a Compulsory Curriculum' (1973)
even went so far as to argue for the justifiability of a uniform
compulsory curriculum on the grounds that it would equip
pupils precisely for the exercise of autonomy.

A threefold analysis of the nature of autonomy has been
fairly widely accepted, embracing the making of independent
judgements (or authenticity), a degree of reflectiveness on the
criteria of judgement and integrity in acting according to one's
judgements.   But the value of this educational aim has been
less easy to explicate, some stressing the paradox of questioning it, some relating it to prudence, while others point to the
establishment of a definite identity or to the personal dignity
that goes with accepting final responsibility for one's life and
actions.   The connections with the conditions which might
best foster its development, and its economic and political
implications are very much open questions.   There is also a
problem of reconciling autonomy with the necessity for authority, both in early learning and at the level of political action.
A varied collection of perspectives on autonomy is contained in
Doyle's 'Educational Judgements' (1973).

Philosophical understanding develops organically and not
aggregatively.   What one later comes to see modifies what
earlier one had thought to have been settled.   In philosophy,
everything connects with everything else.   For example, if

behaviourism was valid as a conception of human beings, then Hirst's distinctive 'form' of 'understanding other people' would disappear and become a part of natural science.   Again, if Skinner was right, then we should have to agree that autonomous man 'has been constructed from our ignorance, and as our understanding increases, the very stuff of which he is composed vanishes'. (16)   To complete the third side of this triangle of relations, if the Hirstian forms were really the irreducible bases of all our knowledge, then would they not be the necessary foundation on which autonomy should be built?

There will surely be a place from time to time in philosophy of education for some limited Lockean underlabouring, clearing the ground a little of weeds and obstacles.   But by contrast with the narrow discussions typical of the linguistic period, there is now much more of a sense of the wholeness of problems.   A survey of all and everything would be too much to ask of anyone, but at least a critical widening of perspective is to be expected as one of the gains from a study of philosophy.   And in so far as the transformation of our understanding affects our conception of the situation, then this will have its pervasive effects on our action too.   For as we think, so we act, in schools and out of them.

V

As to the future, that can hardly be regarded as encouraging. Any discipline benefits from new emphases and new approaches as fresh minds tackle both new and perennial problems, whereas new appointments are now likely to be a rarity or even non-existent.   The schools are likely to be preoccupied with the management of contraction and coping with cuts of one sort or another.   In the absence of any major curricular or institutional innovations to loosen the deeper structures of practice, the perceived needs of practitioners are likely to be increasingly of a narrow and immediate kind, which will create a climate of expectation inimical to the kinds of insight offered by the liberalising disciplines.

It is therefore most unlikely that a major alternative to the present broadly analytic style of doing philosophy of education will emerge in the immediate future, though the linguistic paradigm is likely to have increasingly restricted use.   Fresh attacks will doubtless be made on the perennial problems of aims, curriculum, learning, authority, equality and the relation of theory to practice.   New or newly prominent topics may well become the centre of attention, such as the political control of education, political education, (17) the curriculum and work (18) and the nature of further education.

In such a situation, one benefit that may accrue is that the great dust raised by the activity of the late 1960s and early 1970s will settle and it will be possible to distinguish more clearly the solid shapes from insubstantial phantoms and passing fancies.   Perhaps on a larger timescale it is good for there to be such a rhythm of rapid advance followed by a period of stocktaking and consolidation.

REFERENCES

1 R.S. Peters (1964), 'Education as Initiation' (London, Evans).
2 In R.D. Archambault (ed.) (1965), 'Philosophical Analysis and Education' (London, Routledge & Kegan Paul,), pp. 113-38.
3 P.H. Hirst (1963), Philosophy and Educational Theory, 'British Journal of Educational Studies', 12, 1.
4 Reprinted in R.S. Peters (1977), 'Education and the Education of Teachers' (London, Routledge & Kegan Paul), ch. 7.
5 In J. Doyle (ed.) (1973), 'Educational Judgements' (London, Routledge & Kegan Paul), ch. 14.
6 In T. Pateman (ed.) (1972), 'Counter Course' (Harmondsworth, Penguin), pp. 115-39.
7 E. Gellner (1959), 'Words and Things' (London, Gollancz).
8 See reference 5.
9 J. Wilson (1981), Concepts, Contestability and the Philosophy of Education, 'Journal of Philosophy of Education', 15, 1.
10 In S.C. Brown (ed.) (1975), 'Philosophers Discuss Education' (London, Macmillan), ch. 4.
11 R.K. Elliott (1977), Education and Justification, 'Proceedings of the Philosophy of Education Society', 11.
12 For example, R.K. Elliott (1981), Aestheticism, Imagination and Schooling, 'Journal of Philosophy of Education', 15, 1.
13 D. Gorbutt (1972), The New Sociology of Education, 'Education for Teaching', no. 89.
14 R. Pring (1972), Knowledge out of Control, 'Education for Teaching', no. 89.
15 B.F. Skinner (1974), 'About Behaviourism' (London, Cape), p. 104.
16 B.F. Skinner (1972), 'Beyond Freedom and Dignity' (London, Cape), p. 200.
17 For example, see P.A. White (1979), Work-place Democracy and Political Education, 'Journal of Philosophy of Education', 13.
18 For example, see C. Wringe (1981), Education, Schooling and the World of Work, 'British Journal of Educational Studies', 29, 2.

3 THE IDEA OF A UNIFIED SCIENCE OF EDUCATION

I

In Britain, education as a reflective or theoretical study has
passed through several distinct phases over the last quarter
of a century.   A fairly constant element has been 'method'
studies, by which I mean reflection on the teaching of particular curriculum subjects.   This would include how best to
teach each subject, a review of new approaches, discussion of
changing conceptions and perhaps also some consideration of
the justification for teaching each subject at all.   More recently, elements have been drawn into such studies from the
content and methods of the educational disciplines, such as
psychology, especially as this relates to child development.

So far as the educational disciplines themselves are concerned, in the 1950s these normally comprised only psychology
and history, though alongside these there also existed a more
general area of study somewhat vaguely called 'principles of
education'.   During the 1960s further disciplines were added,
most notably philosophy and sociology, but comparative education and economics of education also developed to a lesser
extent.

During the 1970s came something of a reaction against this
differentiation.   It was felt by some that enthusiastic pursuit
of the disciplines had led educational studies too far from the
needs of practice.   Autonomous disciplines are all very well
if academic standards and academic respectability are the main
things, but how does that feed back into the improvement of
practice?   In the 1980s such usually sceptical questions have
been reinforced by politically required cuts in expenditure,
often based on narrowly utilitarian conceptions of national
need.

Less closely scrutinised than the disciplines of education
have been two hybrid fields of study that arose partly in response to the call for more practical relevance.   These hybrid
fields are curriculum studies and administrative or management
studies.   The first of these is concerned with general and
specific matters in curriculum development while the second is
concerned with institutional organisation and management.
These studies are hybrid in that they may draw upon several
disciplines in an attempted integrating focus on practice.

It can be seen from this brief and highly compressed account
of the recent evolution of educational studies in Britain that
there is nothing there that could be regarded as a unified science of education.   In fact, the very phrase 'science of education' would be likely to arouse suspicions of academic imper-
ialism by some one of the disciplines.   I would now like to
argue that this is not just a curious accident of culture or
history but may well be rooted in certain difficulties of principle.

II

A science of education could not be just unreflective practice.
It would at least have to be an articulate set of judgements
about practice.   More than that, it would have to provide for
the raising and answering of all sorts of questions about those
judgements, such as questions about their validity, truth or
adequacy.   But as soon as these judgements were questioned
and investigated, it would become apparent that different kinds
of question could be asked, each carrying different presuppositions.   Each would imply its own version of what would
count as a good answer and by what method to proceed in
trying to find an answer.

Consider as an example a practice of treating boys and girls
differently in some way in schools.   Is there just one unified
set of questions and answers bearing upon that?   On the contrary, each of the educational disciplines has different questions to ask, quite apart from the many detailed practical
matters which will also bear upon the judgement.   For example, what is the history of the practice?   That may reveal
its original justification, which may no longer be valid.   A
comparative perspective would reveal similarities and dissimilar-
ities in other educational systems and something of their point.
Sociology might be interested in how this practice came to be
taken for granted, or what hidden interests it serves.   Psychology might be interested in the exploration of prejudice,
while philosophy might be concerned with the sense and validity of a claim that there was unjust discrimination or unjustifi-
able inequality.   Considerations such as these make the separateness of the educational disciplines an unassailable epistemological fact, though that is not by itself a justification for
pursuing them of course.   But different sorts of questions
are there to be asked and the answers to them do not constitute a single science.

Nevertheless, it might still be said that a kind of unity can
be found.   In spite of there being different disciplines each
asking different questions, it might be said that they do still
address the same topic, namely some aspect of educational

practice.   A parallel example might be a commercial decision to manufacture a certain product.   In this practical case too there would be many different kinds of question to ask, though not necessarily drawn from disciplines.   What is the market for such a product likely to be?   What competing products are there?   Would the trade unions be co-operative over manufacture?   Would the costs and availability of materials be right?   And so on.   But there would be a unity of purpose throughout this deliberation, deriving from a common aim.   To that extent the contributions to the deliberation would all be integrated by way of commentary on a common proposal.   Could not the various disciplines of education be similarly unified, since education is like commerce at least to this extent: goals are set and means are chosen to their achievement?

One possible sort of integration would not be very satisfactory.   This would be for each of the disciplines to contribute its point of view on every question.   That would not be very profitable for the simple reason that the contribution made would be of very uneven interest and value.   On some questions philosophy might have much to say and psychology little or nothing, and vice versa.   Limited collaboration on specific questions or projects might be fruitful, as it has been on some curriculum projects, but as a general practice this would have little to commend it.   Rather better would be for each discipline to make its own appropriate commentaries directly upon those matters of practice on which it had an interesting contribution to make.

A further complication arises from the fact that when one of the disciplines addresses a practical problem with which it has been presented, it may wish to criticise precisely the identification of the problem.   In the view of the discipline, the problem as posed may not be seen as being the real problem. For example, a school may pose as its problem the disruptive behaviour of its pupils and seek help with a solution in terms of some counselling procedures.   But in a particular case one might judge that that is not the real problem: the real problem, on the contrary, is a highly inappropriate curriculum, or the authority structure of the school.   In short, if the educational disciplines are seen as being subordinately related to practical problems as means or techniques only, then practice and the problems which it poses are immediately placed beyond criticism or reassessment by the disciplines.   That will not do.   Multitudes of examples could be given of progress being made in inquiry only when it was seen that the question was wrongly put and that some quite different way of formulating the problem was far more profitable.   In the history of astronomy, Copernicus is a striking example, followed in philosophy by Kant.

Yet it might be said that unity of inquiry can still be found. All that the previous objection requires is an admission of a certain degree of sophistication in how the problems posed for investigation are to be formulated.   Granted that the aims of practice and the problems posed by practice may require critical reassessment, may not a unified science yet emerge?   But now one has to face the existence of apparently irreconcilable differences in conceptions of education, based on different sets of values and their relative weightings.   To take some historical examples, when Castiglione described the education of the courtier, or John Locke the gentleman, or Rousseau the natural man, they were not indicating different means to a single and agreed end.   Turning to some more contemporary examples, we shall not easily find unity of educational conception as between secular and religious outlooks, or in the latter between Catholicism and Islam.   Again, some people want a liberal education of a traditional kind, whereas others want something much more vocational.   Some emphasise retaining breadth of study, while others want specialisation in depth. And then there is the extremely important dispute, in Britain at least, between those who want some kind of common egalitarian education and those who want different kinds of education to be provided, variously suited to different levels of ability and quality of mind.

It would be no help in the face of this difficulty to turn to some supposedly neutral analysis of the concept of education in the hope of finding a single focus for a unified science. The general concept of education, in contrast to more determinate conceptions, implies little more than some programme of transforming people in their outlook and understanding, their attitudes and values, by means of learning.   But once you begin specifying what is to be learned, in what manner and by whom, then the answers do not constitute a harmonious chorus but point to a diversity of fundamentally different conceptions.   Liberal education differs from education aimed at producing the new socialist man, as does humanistic education from the strictly utilitarian.   Even circumstances produce and justify differing conceptions.   One society finds itself faced with the problem of assimilating or respecting the different cultures of substantial immigrant groups, while another is relatively unaffected by this problem.   One social group may be threatened with the complete loss of national identity unless education is applied to developing a strong consciousness of this, while other groups face no such problem.   Both differences in circumstances and differences in value judgements therefore make it highly implausible to suggest that a single and agreed conception of education is possible.

These differences affect the disciplines themselves in a more intrinsic way.   It is not just that the disciplines are impeded

in their progress towards unity by differing value judgements
about matters outside them.   There are striking differences
of conception within the disciplines themselves.   These differences lead to criticisms of a fundamental kind both within a
given discipline and between the disciplines.   For example,
consider the differences in psychology between Freudians and
behaviourists, or in sociology between the positivist and phenomenological traditions, or in philosophy between empiricists
and existentialists.   If, for example, it was proposed to co-
ordinate the disciplines round a unifying inquiry into disruptive behaviour in the classroom, that project would not get as
far as drawing up an agreed agenda for discussion.

It might be said that at least limited progress can be made
towards constructing a unified science of education by concentrating on the empirical disciplines.   What they report claims
to be, and no doubt sometimes is, true.   If discoveries are
made about the characteristics of children with left-handed-
ness, or the pattern of abilities in some group, then do not
these findings, together with others like them, begin to constitute a science of education?   There are two comments that
I would like to make about that.

First, the relevance of these findings can only become apparent if we assume certain aims to be worthwhile.   Left-handed-
ness, for example, takes on a very different significance if
this preference is permitted or discouraged in a given society.
To give these objective findings educational significance,
therefore, they have to be seen in the light of some educational conception, and these vary.

Furthermore, most if not all of such empirical findings are
true only in a restricted way.   They are true only of certain
groups and not of man as such.   For example, the pattern of
abilities empirically discovered in a given group will be relative to what that group has been taught, and this will in turn
once again reflect different valuations and conceptions.   Child
development studies may be similarly restricted.   This restriction in range of application may be true more obviously of
philosophy and history of education, which explicitly study
the implications of particular conceptions and their institutional
embodiment.   These arguments do not show that truth is not
discovered by the disciplines, but that its range of application
may be restricted and may therefore lack relevance to other
educational conceptions.

If I may now draw together the difficulties that I have
noticed in considering the idea of a unified science of education, they are as follows.   First, the separateness of the
various educational disciplines is an unassailable epistemological
fact, though that does not by itself preclude every kind of

unified endeavour.   Next, the contributions to a given problem which the disciplines might make would be very uneven.
Furthermore, seen from the point of view of one of the disciplines, the problem posed to it might itself call for reassessment or reformulation.   Even so, these points would not
necessarily preclude a unified inquiry.   Much more serious,
however, is the evident fact that conceptions of education
differ greatly according to the differing sets of values and
their relative weightings which underlie each conception.
And these divergences are not just external to the disciplines
as problems which they outwardly face, but enter into the
very conception of the discipline itself and its proper methods
of inquiry.   Finally, the truths discovered by the disciplines
may be restricted in their relevance to particular conceptions
of education.   It is for all these reasons that I ventured the
suspicion at the outset that the lack of a unified science of
education in Britain was not just a curious accident of history
or culture, but could well be rooted in difficulties of principle.

III

It will be clear from this that I do not myself think that any
unity of educational conception can be found by sitting down
and endeavouring to be ruled only by rational considerations.
If physical scientists and engineers sit down and deliberate,
or better still get up and experiment, they are likely to
arrive at the same or converging solutions even though they
work far apart and in isolation from one another.   This is
because the empirical world is one.   But the world of human
ideals and values is diverse and there is no reason to suppose
that educational theorists, even granted an actual desire to
collaborate, would be guided to the same conclusions if only
they gave their minds seriously to thinking through the question of educational values.   Quite apart from the apparently
insuperable problems created by divergent value judgements,
there is the diversity of empirical human nature, for example
the differences in the speed and complexity of what individuals
can learn, and in temperament and personality.

A radical solution to the problem of diversity of educational
conceptions that has been proposed is strikingly simple.   It
is simply that schools should withdraw from the business of
educating and concentrate instead on training in utilitarian
skills.   But this is too simple.   For one thing, even the
selection and the manner of transmission of such skills rests
on, and by participation transmits, certain values.   For
another thing, education will still continue, though informally,
in the home, through the media and at the workplace.   Why
should it be supposed that the results of these informal influ-

ences are to be preferred to a carefully considered programme of public education?   Liberty for the learner is as much infringed in parental as it is in school education.

Another solution, at least at the practical level, is to cut through all divergences with a politically imposed uniformity of practice.   This might be achieved either by a diversity of school systems each of which represents a single educational conception, as when churches are allowed to establish their own schools, or more drastically by an overall national conception centrally imposed by the government.   In each case, limited kinds of research would still be possible without violating autonomous intellectual standards, but research would have to be denied any opportunity to question either the terms in which problems were posed or the presupposed aims that were being pursued.   This would result in inquiry which was unified only by a ruling which was intellectually arbitrary.   And the corresponding educational practice would probably be engaged in indoctrination.

There is perhaps yet one more possibility and it is one which has gained much though by no means complete support amongst English-speaking philosophers of education.   This is to develop the idea of the individual as an autonomous chooser with a recognised right to construct his own life within wide moral limits.   The inquiry then investigates what knowledge, understanding and type of character would be implicit in such an educational conception.   The content of learning may in this way be divided between what is presupposed by being a well-informed chooser and what must be regarded as more optional and indeed subject to the pupil's choice.   Methods of teaching have correspondingly to distinguish between what can be straightforwardly a matter of instruction and what calls for more tentative modes of presentation.   There is also a tendency to emphasise the formal features of the various subjects, such as their methods and general criteria, rather than their specific and more changeable content.

This conception of education seeks agreement in agreement to differ.   It tries to accommodate diversity by restraining any particular conception from decisive influence and instead allowing choice or commitment to follow upon a progressively developing understanding of alternatives.   It is a liberal conception of education.   But it too has its critics, who reveal it as just as much involving a substantive conception of educational values as do other conceptions, in spite of its second-order character.   This would make the liberal conception one amongst other conceptions all competing for allegiance, with none apparently having a clear intellectual right to claim precedence over the rest, or any right to claim to be the proper focus for a single unified science of education.

My general conclusion, then, is this.   Only in restricted
and partial ways can there be a science of education.   A
single and unified science is precluded by differences in educational values which select different ranges of discovered
fact as being of practical importance.   Furthermore, these
differences of conception are not just something external to
the disciplines but, on the contrary, enter into the very conception of the disciplines themselves.   The most obvious way
of overcoming these obstacles to a unified science would be
to impose a politically directed uniformity on educational research.   But that would, from an intellectual point of view,
be an arbitrary solution, and the absence of such uniformity
may therefore be regarded as progress rather than with
despair.

4 EDUCATION AND POLITICS

Can education be kept out of politics?   The question is not a
new one, although the frequency with which it is raised may
be obscured by its taking other forms.   We might instead be
asked whether the state should control the curriculum, or
whether the curriculum can be politically neutral.   Sometimes
the ensuing answers give detailed considerations for or against
the desirability of government directives on what should be
taught.   Such arguments are offered against the background
of a particular society at a particular historical juncture - but
other answers are more sweeping.   These more sweeping
answers invite us to agree that the state *cannot* be neutral
regarding the curriculum, or more simply that education
cannot be kept out of politics, whatever anyone might wish or
think desirable in the matter.   These 'cannots' and 'musts'
pre-empt the more particular debates and attempt to bulldoze
the contending parties into a single corner.

Are such coercive attempts successful?   Is it the case that
we 'can only' view the curriculum from a political perspective?
Evidently Richard Norman is one of those who would answer
affirmatively here, although it is unclear from his article
whether he recognises there to be a distinction between ethics
and politics.   He writes: 'questions about what to teach and
how to teach it can be answered only in the context of some
political perspective or other.' (1)   Thus such questions *can
only* be answered ... etc.   Some filling out of this necessity
is provided by John White who writes: 'decisions about curriculum framework are inescapably connected with *political*
[his italics] views about the nature of the Good Society.' (2)
The supporting argument is that curricular learning affects
the kind of society which comes to be, that such learning
therefore implies a view of the good society, that such a view
is a political view and that as such it must be settled by political decision and cannot be left to educational professionals.
Thus curricular decisions are *inescapably* political.

Is all this a fairy story or must we indeed bow to the inevitable and so cease to engage in the more particular debates
about desirability or undesirability?   For if curricular decisions 'can only' be made from a political perspective, or if
they are 'inescapably' political, then those more particular
debates will be on a par with arguing the desirability or

undesirability of bachelors being married, of two and two
making five, or of children learning algebra before they learn
arithmetic.   To pinpoint the concern of my opening question:
can education be kept out of politics?

Perhaps a first reaction to this question would be to say
that it all depends on what you mean by the 'political', and
certainly it is a common enough view of philosophical argument
that it must at least begin by a definition of terms.   However, such a view is open to familiar enough objections, if it
is taken quite generally.   The demand for definitions leads
to a regress, since the terms in which the definition is given
will themselves be undefined.   Again, some terms are clearly
indefinable in other terms anyway, such as colours or sounds;
and it cannot be the case that we must first be provided with
a definition if we are clearly to mean something, since unless
we already had at least a notion of the meaning we would have
no way of recognising whether or not the proposed definition
was correct. (3)   Serious reservations are therefore in order
if at the outset we are always pressed to furnish definitions,
but that is not to say that something of the sort is never
profitable;   and in the case of the 'political' some preliminary
clarification is very desirable.   Just as with the question 'Is
morality relative?', so too with 'Can education be kept out of
politics?', much futility and argument at cross-purposes are
caused by omitting first to attempt at least some clarificatory
attention to the key term, in this case not 'relative' but
'political'.

Politics, of course, is not only found in the activities of the
state.   There are political aspects to all institutions, for example to the school and even the family.   Anyone in a school
who is concerned through the exercise of authority or power
to revise its form of organisation, or its allocation of resources, or its hierarchy of authority is concerned with a form of
politics.   The political, it may suffice us to say, is concerned
with ruling decisions on such matters as the allocation of resources, the regulation of competing interests, the establishment or reform of certain institutions, the determination of
priorities in such contexts and the ends of such activities.
It implies a theory and in turn a particular ethical or social
philosophical view on certain matters of value.   Thus it
couples a perspective on justice, power, liberty, happiness
and so on with a particular social analysis, yielding principles
and policies to guide the action of some ruling authority or
power.   Politics is found not only at the level of the state,
but it is that level which presently concerns us.   Thus, once
again, and with this attempt at clarification (although hardly
definition) in mind: can education be kept out of politics?

Concerning any activity within a state, we may say that it

is either permitted (perhaps even enforced) or not permitted,
and in that trivial sense the state cannot be neutral towards
it.   This is as true of seeking a job as it is of taking the
dog for a walk.   Concerning children's education more particularly, states typically require of children that they be
educated, whether in institutions provided for that purpose
by the state itself or by private provision.   I doubt that it
is actually inescapable that the state should have such a requirement, but on various grounds it is very desirable and it
is typically featured in lists of human rights.   I draw attention to this massive infringement of children's liberty, with its
denial of early economic independence and its placing of the
child under some pedagogic authority, not in order to discuss
its validity but simply to indicate one way in which the state
is already involved in education.   Anyone who raises the
question of whether education can be kept out of politics
while supposing that up to now politics has not been so involved is therefore very mistaken indeed.

He is very much mistaken in another way too.   If he should
concentrate his attention on education as the transmission of
knowledge and understanding, which is indeed the heart of it,
then it may go unnoticed that such transmission, beyond a
very elementary stage, requires a material basis.   It requires
buildings, equipment, books, materials and teachers, all of
which must be financed in some way.   Such resources are
always in scarce supply in the sense that they are provided
from an always limited overall stock of wealth.   In considering the normal case, that of the financing of the state's own
educational institutions, the allocation of resources to education
has to compete with allocations to such other desirable services
as defence, law enforcement, public health and government
itself.   Thus provision of the material basis for the state's
educational activities is inescapably political at some level,
even if it is only that of a block provision the further division
of which, or the more specific purposes of which, are left to
others to decide.   Thus once again we may say that the
bearing of politics upon education is no new or boldly revolu-
tionary proposal, but is already a large everyday reality.

What more is there to be said?   We have already seen that
the actuality is a massive political infringement of personal
liberty and a global political control over the allocation of re-
resources;   but there are those who would argue that beyond
this politics not only should not but actually cannot go. (4)
The argument employed to substantiate this remarkable claim
is as follows.   Education is concerned with knowledge and
understanding (as indeed it is).   Knowledge and understanding take various forms each of which embodies criteria of truth
and standards of excellence which are autonomous.   Such
criteria and standards derive from the nature of the subject-

matter and not from any political authority.   Thus science is
properly governed by truth criteria which make reference to
experimentally controlled observation and by standards of excellence such as simplicity and explanatory power.   Scientific
thinking is thus governed by autonomous criteria and standards and can only be distorted from its true nature by the
intrusion of political requirements, the usual warning example
of which is Lysenko's version of biology.

Much the same point can be made about art.   If artistic
activity was governed by political requirements, then we might
well find such absurdities as the pedestrian compositions of
some politically approved hack being aesthetically preferred to
the vastly superior compositions of someone else on the
grounds that the former had the right class credentials whereas the latter was 'bourgeois'.   Even political education itself,
if it is to be education and not indoctrination, must have a
certain autonomy in relation to particular political theories and
practices.   It must be free to establish truth according to
appropriate autonomous criteria.   To put the point epigramma-
tically, we might say that truth is independent of the will.
It depends on how things are and not on how political authority might wish them to be.   Thus if we are concerned truly
to educate, these autonomous criteria and standards must be
respected and therefore a fence exists which politics cannot
cross.   In this sense, education must be kept out of politics.

Indeed in that sense it must be;   but that is very far from
saying that politics cannot go beyond the matters of personal
liberty and material provision that have already been noticed.
Compatibly with respecting the autonomous criteria and standards which were mentioned, political authority could require
certain subjects to be included in the curriculum and certain
others to be excluded from it, or certain topics within those
subjects to be included or excluded.   Consider the intended
difference between university and polytechnical education in
the so-called 'binary system' (I do not refer to the actual difference, or its absence).   The intention, and it was a political intention, was that polytechnics should provide more specifically for skilled roles in industry and administration,
whereas university education would retain its general character.   Again, consider a decision to give much greater weight
to mathematics, science and modern languages, perhaps at the
expense of social studies, classics, art or history.   That is a
possible political decision which nevertheless respects the
autonomy of mathematics, history, etc.   As a result of our
entry into the Common Market, the government might wish to
see much greater prominence given to the teaching of modern
languages, and all this without violation of the maxim that
truth is independent of the will.   Therefore the argument
that politics cannot impinge on education beyond the matters

of personal liberty and material provision is not made out.
Political authority, that is to say government, could go much
further quite compatibly with respecting those sorts of autonomy which are constitutive of the different forms of knowledge
and understanding.   You can appoint, or sack, or change
the hours of a teacher of Spanish without presuming to dictate
what is good Spanish, what is excellent in Spanish literature
or even how Spanish should be taught.   Even if there is an
attempt to derive certain restrictions from the concept of education, there would still remain a considerable latitude for
variations in exclusion, inclusion and weighting.

Granted that the political agenda could be more embracing in
this way, must it be so?   Are there further arguments to
show that the curriculum cannot be politically neutral, and so
must be brought under political control?   It can hardly be
doubted that many curricular decisions made by professionals
are politically neutral in their intention, but the question is
whether those decisions can be neutral in their effects.   It
may plausibly be argued that, whatever our intention, none
of our actions is ever politically neutral in its effects, *a for-
tiori* none of the curricular decisions of educational professionals can be neutral in their effects - but it may not be
immediately apparent why this must be so.

Consider first the case of a headteacher faced with a NUPE
caretakers' strike.   The headteacher may well wish to remain
politically neutral in relation to this strike (especially as the
goodwill of caretakers is much to be prized).   However, the
caretaker refuses to unlock the school gates, without which
the pupils cannot get into school.   Now either the headteacher
opens the gates himself or he does not.   If he does he acts
in a way which minimises the effectiveness of the strike;   if
he does not then he maximises that effectiveness.   He cannot
be neutral.   Next, consider a teacher's curricular decision as
to whether he will deliberately aim to counter racialist attitudes
in his class.   Racialism is a political matter and either he
takes a decision on it or he does not.   If he does, that is a
political commitment of one sort or another;   if he does not,
then he leaves unopposed all those social forces which are
nevertheless powerfully acting on his pupils to form in them
attitudes related to this issue, and again he cannot be neutral.
Once more, consider a lecturer called upon to cancel his lecture as there is to be a political meeting by the students.
Whether he cancels the lecture or he does not, his action has
a certain political significance: it either impedes or facilitates
attendance at the meeting.

These examples can now be generalised, as follows.   Every
curricular decision has an effect on the eventual pattern of
educatedness with which pupils emerge from their schooling.

They are, as a result, better or worse informed, more or less
skilled, sensitive or insensitive, caring or uncaring in some
respect.   All of this either will or will not harmonise with,
impede or facilitate, a given political vision of the desirable
society.   Through its effect on the resulting patterns of
educatedness, and through the relevance of that to a political
vision, curricular decisions are therefore unavoidably political
in significance and should therefore be brought under political
control by the state.   Thus the argument might go.

What are we to make of this argument?   Has all talk of the
desirability or undesirability of political control been successfully pre-empted by the disclosure of an unavoidable necessity?   Let us first register the potential scope and force of
this form of argument by an extension employing parity of
reasoning.   The school may be the formal educational agency
in the modern state but there is also a multitude of informal
agencies.   For example, the family, factory, the office, the
media, indeed every aspect of life has some educative or mis-
educative influence.   All of these agencies affect our knowledge, understanding, sensitivity, skills and what we care
about.   The idealist tradition in philosophy, as exemplified
by such men as Hegel, Bradley, Bosanquet, Green and indeed
Dewey, has shown the most vivid awareness of these facts. (5)
Granted the facts, does the argument, by parity of reasoning,
mean that *every aspect of life* must be brought under political control?   Perhaps it does, but for the moment let us be
content just to register the extent of the implications of
accepting this form of argument and turn to another point.

Even if the argument were accepted, it would still be possible for an educational programme to be neutral as between
rival political theories.   This could happen not because the
programme was politically irrelevant in its bearings but
because it was equally relevant to all the contending political
theories.   As others have pointed out, political control of
the curriculum by a particular political party in office does
not necessarily mean that the curriculum would then become a
political football.   If the politically enforced curriculum required the teaching of such 'basics' as mathematics, science,
physical education and morality then it might be equally
acceptable, granted certain further specifications of actual
content, to all the parties concerned.   Agreement on some
ends is possible, and further agreement is possible on common
means to diverse ends.   Arithmetic is as useful for book-
keeping in the commune as it is for calculating profit and loss,
while gratitude for freely rendered kindness is thought appropriate by all.   Thus at least a degree of party political neutrality is possible in that a curricular core might be desired
by all.   Of course, enforcing it would be like requiring
teachers to breathe, or to wear clothes in cold weather, or to
eat some food from time to time, but that is another matter.

However, all of this might be said to be so much skirmish-
ing.   Is it possible to face the argument (let us name it the
'totalitarian argument') without at once being knocked flat?
The totalitarian argument rests on a major assumption, which
is this.   If any act has a political significance through the
bearing of its consequences, then *ipso facto* that significance
must take precedence over any other.   For without that
assumption, the significance might indeed be there for those
monomaniac enough forever to be ferreting it out, but that
would not justify the conclusion that *control* is necessary.
It must be assumed that political significance must take precedence over significance of any other sort for this necessity
of control to follow.   For example, on purely commercial
grounds it may seem best to site some new installation in Newtown but this would ignore the significance of the unemployment situation in Oldtown, where matters are truly desperate.
The politically overriding decision is therefore taken, perhaps
reasonably enough, to require, or to supply inducements for,
a choice of Oldtown as the site.

Should the political significance always be thus overriding?
Consider another case.   A student is to have a last-minute
and personally very important tutorial on her research before
returning to some distant place where she will complete the
writing up unsupervised;   but the students' union has called
for a demonstration against some aspect of government policy
and the demonstration clashes with the unchangeable time for
the tutorial.   Does furthering the political cause by adding a
mite to the size of a very large crowd automatically override
the massive personal significance of the last-minute tutorial?
Surely there is at least the logical space for a negative
answer here? - but if so, then what is the status of the totalitarian assumption?

I said earlier that concerning any activity within a state,
either the state permits it or it does not, and in that sense
the state cannot be neutral towards it.   Thus in a formal and
often extremely trivial sense every act has political significance, but in a more substantive sense this may not be so.
For a political theory may incorporate in itself the view that
the agenda of matters deserving of government control should
be limited.   Let us call this the 'liberal' position, simply in
the sense that it deliberately chooses to leave certain areas of
activity free from political intervention.   Formally those activities still have political significance (they are permitted) but
substantively they do not (they are not on the agenda).   The
items thus excluded might, so far as I can see, include many
concerning education.   Of course, schools would still produce
patterns of educatedness in children and these patterns would
still have an effect on the kind of society that came to be.
The same would be true of the informal educative effects of

the family, the factory, the office, the media and so on.
However, the political principle could still be operative that
such influences and their effects should be excluded from
substantive political control or attention.   The existence of a
measure of autonomy in educational institutions could itself be
part of the vision of a good society.

Various grounds for such a possibility can be imagined.
They might be economic, as when it is thought that children's
education is more properly a matter for private rather than
for public expenditure.   They might be prudential, as when
control over education is not sought by a political party since
loss of office would leave an already constructed highway open
for an unwanted control to be exercised by political opponents.
Where political education is specifically concerned, the grounds
might be epistemic, in that it might be recognised that these
matters are controversial and that each individual must judge
for himself in due course.

I am not concerned here with arguing whether the state
ought or ought not to assume control over the curriculum, but
with the pre-emptive question of whether the state *must* assume
control, because this is 'inescapable'. or because curricular
questions 'can only' be settled in the context of some substantive political perspective or other - and I suggest that this
logical or conceptual coercion does not exist.   Government
does not have to be totalitarian, although the decision not to
be so is of course itself political.   Thus there are *choices*,
and the terms in which the debate over state control should
therefore be conducted are those of should and should not,
desirable and undesirable.   We are not forced into submission
by a logical half-nelson here.

If that is right, then I would expect the debate to continue
with reference to such considerations as the actual use or
abuse of their freedom made by the professionals, the place of
experiment, the centralisability of relevant knowledge, co-
ordination or the lack of it as this bears on geographical
mobility, effects on equality of opportunity, effects on professional self-esteem, the possible need for more accountability
to the public, the lessons to be learned from foreign examples,
the vocational relevance of the curriculum, the responsiveness
of schools to social needs, and so on.   The upshot would be
an historically relative verdict, based on how matters were
developing at a particular place and time with professionals of
a certain quality.   In such more particular discussions a
word of caution may not be out of place: is it not extraordi-
narily naive to suppose, as seems sometimes to be supposed,
that if state control were secured then of course it would be
one's own vision that would be implemented, or that the political forces thus born would be as readily kept under control as

the political ideas that were marshalled in one's head?   Perhaps the fate of the sorcerer's apprentice should at least be borne in mind when we deal with the political.

There one might feel inclined to leave the matter, so far as the possibility, if not the desirability, of keeping the curriculum out of politics is concerned.   There is, however, a rather disconcerting line of argument that has not yet been considered.   It starts by drawing our attention to an assumption that I have been making throughout, namely that what has to be considered is the direct influence of government on the educational programme and hence on the pattern of educatedness that eventually emerges.   Suppose that that possible source of influence is held in check in accordance with a theory of limited government, which would be the 'liberal' position in the sense that I gave to it.   Does education then proceed in a political vacuum?   What then happens, it might be argued, is that the existing state of affairs is unopposed in its influence in forming political attitudes and we therefore have a species of conservatism.   Not having certain items on the agenda does not make them just go away, or prevent them from having any influence.

This might, of course, be unexceptionable even though true. Political parties might take a swings-and-roundabouts view of their gains and losses and decide to settle for such a state of affairs.   However, such bland acceptance is unlikely to be forthcoming from a Marxist theory based on an historical analysis in terms of class struggle and class domination.   (I ignore here the many differences which exist within the broad band of theories that might be called 'Marxist'.)   What does not appear on the agenda of one political theory may be central to the agenda of another.   Such an alternative theory might see both an overt and a hidden curriculum busily at work from the first, and throughout schooling, inculcating politically significant attitudes.   Schooling would be seen as inculcating attitudes of deference to authority appropriate to a class-divided society.   It would be seen as giving apparent legitimacy to unequal distributions of wealth, status and power through fallacious conceptions of equality of opportunity. Schooling would furthermore be seen as tranquillising political consciousness by distracting attention from real class interests by occupying time with harmless subjects like ancient history and nature study.   Thus by the time that school-leaving age is reached, the actual arrangements in the society will have so far come to seem rational and inevitable that a Marxist analysis will then seem highly implausible.   An imaginative appreciation of how very different things might be will have been pre-empted by solidifying consciousness round the actual. To see schooling in terms of such a political significance as this (and other, non-Marxist arguments in the same style

might be advanced in terms of other political theories) is not
just to be monomaniac in ferreting out merely formal and
trivial political significance, but to draw attention to what are
taken to be really substantive political issues concerning
interests which could scarcely be outweighed by interests of
any other sort.   Who has drawn up the liberal's limited
agenda anyway?

How far one is disconcerted by this line of argument and
how far one thinks that proposals must be forthcoming to
meet it will no doubt largely depend upon how credible one
finds it.   It is at the very least interesting.   One thing
that might be done, although it would be an impossibly large
task to do more than adumbrate here, would be precisely to
consider the truth of each of these claims.   Is there a
coherent ruling class which dominates the majority in its own
exploitative interests?   Are the kinds of attitude towards
authority and the inequalities of achievement which the school
is said to bring about simply devices of domination, or are
they to be found in all industrialised societies, perhaps being
derivative from certain intractable features of human nature
and difference and from the necessities of efficient production?   The criticism that holding out real equality of opportunity to all is contradicted by the unchanging proportion of
'better jobs', no matter how hard pupils may strive, seems
logically sound, yet on the other hand there is at least some
small degree of class mobility in society.   In short, how far
is it true that the school 'reflects' class divisions in some way
which is of pressingly urgent political significance?   I do not
intend that question as being merely rhetorical.

The least that would seem to be called for by way of a proposal, and it is a proposal with much else to be said for it
too, is that more attention should be given to political education itself.   To be compatible with what was said earlier
about autonomous criteria and standards, such political education would have to be uncommitted, at least in any institution-
ally reinforced way, to any one political theory.   Perhaps it
would have to be concerned with some kind of basic 'political
literacy', to use Crick's term. (6)   It would stand in much
the same case as religious education in dealing with very controversial issues and often incompatible alternatives, and in
raising puzzles about a supposedly 'neutral' teacher.

However, working out the implications of such a proposal as
that would be a separate task in its own right.   My purpose
in this paper has been simply to deny the existence of any
supposed logical or conceptual necessities which would effectively pre-empt all discussion of the contingent desirability of
state control.   There are no such necessities.   We are free
to choose the nature and extent of the control which the state

should exercise according to such considerations as may seem best at some particular historical juncture.

POSTSCRIPT

At the time this article was being written, the question was being raised of the permissibility of athletes participating in the Olympic Games at Moscow.   Many of the arguments which I discussed regarding education could have been formulated in an entirely parallel way for sport, and it may assist in deciding whether those arguments are valid if some of the parallels are indicated.

Much of the debate in the case of sport, just as with education, is misdirectedly occupied with the supposed political neutrality of sport, a principal point here being the apolitical intentions of the sportsmen themselves.   However, whether the sportsmen participate or they do not, and regardless of their intentions, their actions have political significance through their effects.   The Games provide a vehicle for various manifestations of national prestige;   pointed absence could affect the prestige of the Soviet government with its own people, participation could open a rather closed society to a much wider public, Soviet dissidents would feel encouraged or discouraged, and so on.   In the longer term there might be effects on the likelihood of further Soviet military activity or on the readiness of states to use the Games themselves as a political instrument.

Again, and just as with education, states can already be seen to be involved heavily in sport, for example in controlling the liberty of citizens as to which sports will be permitted (not gladiatorial combat, and perhaps not certain kinds of animal hunting or baiting), and in providing the material basis of sporting activities (stadia, sports complexes, training facilities).   Even the manner of engaging in sport may be affected as with the Chinese principle of 'friendship first, competition second'.

However, there are certain aspects of sport which have to be recognised as autonomous, just as certain aspects of scientific or aesthetic education have to be recognised as autonomous.   For example, there is the place of various kinds of fairness in competition, stylistic values in judging gymnastics, diving or skating, and the values specifically constitutive of excellence in any given sport.   If judges of diving took the diver's nationality into account, the result for that sport would be like that of giving precedence to political requirements in formulating a biological theory, as with Lysenko. The recognition of such a degree of autonomy would neverthe-

less be quite compatible with extensive political control over
many aspects of sporting activity.

As with education, so with sport, the upshot is the same.
The state *can* exercise various forms of control but it is a
logically open question whether it *should*.   A decision here is
not pre-empted simply by the fact of sport having political
significance.   If it had not been for Afghanistan, there
would still have been much of political significance in going to
Moscow, but presumably every state that had allowed its
Olympic Committee to agree to that choice of site had tacitly
taken the view that the political significance was not overriding.   Had Russia at the same time as Afghanistan sent
troops into Yugoslavia, Iran, Pakistan, Finland and Turkey,
then presumably very few (although assuredly some) states
would have countenanced their athletes going to Moscow.
Circumstances alter cases, and the point is that we are not
faced with having to bow to a logical inevitability but are
called upon to make a substantive choice;   and what that
logically open choice should be will depend on a multitude of
contingent factors.

REFERENCES

1 Norman, R. (1975), The neutral teacher?, in Brown, S.C.
   (ed.), 'Philosophers Discuss Education' (London, Macmillan),
   p. 187.
2 White, J.P. (1976), Teacher accountability, 'Proceedings of
   the Philosophy of Education Society', 10, p. 64.
3 These points about definition are interestingly elaborated
   upon in Best, D. (1978), 'Philosophy and Human Movement'
   (London, Unwin), pp. 88-90.
4 See, for example, Wilson, J. (1979), 'Preface to Philosophy
   of Education' (London, Routledge & Kegan Paul).
5 For a very interesting substantiation of this point see
   Gordon, P. and White, J. (1979), 'Philosophers as Educational Reformers' (London, Routledge & Kegan Paul).
6 Crick, B. and Porter, A. (eds) (1978), 'Political Education
   and Political Literacy' (London, Longmans).

Part two
ASPECTS OF THE CURRICULUM

5 BALANCE AND COHERENCE: SOME CURRICULAR PRINCIPLES IN RECENT REPORTS

I

There are many pressures currently operating which invite a reconsideration of the curriculum as a whole, especially the secondary school curriculum.   Examples of such pressures include falling numbers of pupils and cutbacks in the number of teachers, both of which compel decisions concerning priorities and invite the attempt to identify 'essentials' or a 'core' which must be protected from the vagaries of staff changes. Again, the composition of governing bodies has, following the Taylor Report, (1) been reviewed, which raises the question of who should determine the curriculum and indeed what the terms of reference for governing bodies should be in this connection.   Something vaguely called 'national need', a notion as imprecise as it is thought to be important, has also been cited in support of calls for a review.   National need has also been claimed specifically to justify the intervention of the Secretary of State in determining the curriculum. (2)

Elements of such a reconsideration of the curriculum as a whole have appeared in a spate of recent official documents, such as the Green Paper 'Education in Schools' (3) and the HMI surveys 'Primary Education in England' (4) and 'Aspects of Secondary Education in England'. (5)   The government's call for a framework has been met by the DES document 'A Framework for the Curriculum' (6) and by the Inspectorate, speaking with a voice distinguishable from that of the DES, in 'A View of the Curriculum'. (7)   Most recent of all is 'The School Curriculum', (8) which represents the government's own firm conclusions for curricular action arising out of the Great Debate.   Yet further documents are promised.

With such a fundamental review in prospect, one might expect that equally fundamental curricular principles would be discussed.   Setting to one side the administrative question of who should determine the curriculum, the principles that I have in mind are those which should properly determine the construction of the curriculum, whoever may do the constructing.   In the event, an explicit discussion of fundamental principles is not quite what has occurred.   'Primary Education in England', for example, sought to retain the breadth and elements of the existing curriculum though with a caution about French, and concentrated instead on weaknesses in science and stimulating the more able pupils.   'Aspects of Secondary Education in England' raised questions about the extent to which options amongst subjects should be allowed, and advocated that a larger number of subjects (though not necessarily syllabi) should be common to all pupils.

If we turn from the Inspectorate's reports to the views of the DES, a statement of general aims was made in 'Education in Schools' (9) and subsequently repeated both in 'A Framework for the Curriculum' (10) and in 'The School Curriculum' (11) (with the exception of the reference in the first document to esteeming the role of industry - an aim which had struck some people as begging the question in assuming that every aspect of industry was actually worthy of such unquestioning esteem).   But this set of aims was never put to work in any way that was visibly generative of the curricular recommendations that followed.

Anything that might reasonably be called a fundamental curricular principle has been hard to find in all this, but there are at least two possible candidates which have pervasively appeared in recent discussions and which merit some attention. These are 'balance' and 'coherence'.   My own view is that both of these notions have work to do, but whether they can work quite as hard as they have been expected to do is more open to question.   They seem rather to be secondary principles, not just in the sense that it is in discussions of the secondary curriculum that they have mostly appeared, but also in a further sense to which I shall draw attention in what follows.   What I propose to do in this paper, then, is to consider the merits specifically of balance and coherence as curricular principles.

II

'Aspects of Secondary Education in England' contains the following statement:

> the subjects available were grouped in such a way that in
> any one option 'block' they were confined to one particular
> area of the curriculum;   one 'block' might consist exclusively
> of sciences, another of social studies, another of crafts and
> so on.   Such a structured system was designed to achieve
> a 'balanced' curriculum by ensuring that all or most areas
> of the curriculum were included in each pupil's programme.
> ... In some schools, however, the word 'balance' was used
> more loosely, and a 'balanced' programme was one in which
> the essential subjects were those thought to have vocational
> importance or significance for higher education, which were

then 'balanced' by a subject or subjects from a different, otherwise absent, area of the curriculum. (12)

These contrasting references to balance bring out the first point that I would like to make about this principle, namely that it assumes prior judgements as to the elements between which you are to find a balance. In the passage quoted, both an apparently liberal and a more vocational orientation of the curriculum are expressed in terms of finding a balance. But a balance could intelligibly be sought and found in endless varying combinations of elements: between French and ancient Chinese, for example, or between snap and tiddly-winks. More seriously, a balance is often sought in a very wide range of contexts, such as between theory and practice in initial training, between direction and choice in learning, between sexes and abilities in a comprehensive school intake and between coursework and formal examination in assessment. Given the instruction 'construct a balanced curriculum', you could not even begin to do this until constituent elements had been furnished from elsewhere, their worth having been justified by reference to some other unstated principles.

But suppose that one had a list of such elements. Where would a balance between them lie? Would equal weight need to be given to each, as the metaphor would seem to imply if taken literally? A balanced diet does not consist of equal parts by weight of each essential foodstuff; it includes *sufficent* of each of the necessary elements. It is no more to be expected that a balanced curriculum will include equal amounts of science and swimming, or mathematics and poetry. Thus one is not surprised to find 'Aspects of Secondary Education in England' stating that 'considering the balance of the whole curriculum, it seems more reasonable to ask for "double-subject" time for science in years 4 and 5'. (13)

This indeterminacy of weighting is explicitly noticed in Schools Council Working Paper 55:

Balance should not, however, be thought of in terms of equal quantities; the balance referred to here is a judicial balance rather than a mathematical one. Behind the judgement lie estimates of minimum requirements, legitimate weightings and special justifications - all, of course, varying according to the professional view taken in the light of particular circumstances. (14)

Thus 'balance' can be seen to be a controversial principle not only in that it takes for granted the elements between which a balance is to be found, but also in that it is very much a matter of judgement how much of each element must be present for us to recognise that a balance has been struck.

Yet a further aspect of balance as a curricular principle is brought out in Schools Council Working Paper 53.   This paper states that 'the case for balance is closely related to that for breadth'. (15)   To some extent this much would seem to be a matter of logic.   For a balance to be struck there must be at least two things between which the balance is found.   But concerning the curriculum, logic alone would not help us in answering the necessary questions as to when we have a satisfactory breadth of studies.   'Aspects of Secondary Education in England' quotes a boy who took English, mathematics, religious education, physical education, physics, chemistry, computer studies, geology and metalwork as an example of *im*balance.   A similar judgement of imbalance was passed on a girl who took English, mathematics, religious education, physical education, home economics, careers, typing, shorthand and commerce.   The objection was that they had dropped history, geography, all aesthetic subjects and in the case of the girl all science. (16)

Does the breadth that is correlative to balance therefore require pupils to sample all of the Hirstian forms, or Phenix's realms?   Should it be thought of in terms of attention to both arts and sciences?   Should it apply also within a single subject area, as when both traditional and modern mathematics are included, or reading, writing, speaking and listening are all present in language work, or 'science' covers physics, chemistry and biology?   One version of how balance and breadth should be related was contained in the Green Paper 'Education in Schools':

The balance and breadth of each child's course is crucial at all school levels ... the offer of options and the freedom to choose do lead some boys and girls to abandon certain areas of study at an early age ... alongside English and mathematics, science should find a secure place for all pupils at least to the age of 16, and that a modern language should do so for as high a proportion as practicable. (17)

This opposition between balance and options is a theme to which I shall return.

If the instruction 'construct a balanced curriculum' tells us neither the range of elements, nor the weighting of each of them, nor yet how broad a range of elements is needed, then what help does it give?   With these dimensions of indeterminacy to the principle, it would seem that exactly the same curricular provision could be seen as either balanced or unbalanced, depending on differing prior commitments, so where is the constraint in this as a principle?   Is it not so flexible as to be no principle at all?   What can be said, I think, is that appeals to balance are often closely connected with justice,

taken as meaning giving what is due.   It is very important
to give what is due, and thus recognise the rights of legitimate claimants, but notoriously justice is hard to locate uncontroversially.

In the curricular case, justice needs to be done to various
elements of possible curricular provision but in this case as in
the other a presupposed set of rights would need to be agreed
before justice could be done.   The characteristic proper function of pleas for balance is therefore to draw attention to the
claim of some curricular element which is in danger of going
unrecognised.   Characteristic temptations to overlook that
claim will spring from a desire to narrow the range in the
interest of specialisation, or by offering too much as optional,
or by concentrating too exclusively on 'basics', yet in drawing
attention to claims, however, we do indeed presuppose that
those claims have had the case for their validity separately
made out.

III

Whereas appeals to balance as a curricular principle exist in
luxuriant profusion, 'coherence' has been more a term of art.
Until quite recently it was only in connection with the proliferation of modular courses at college level that the term made
much of an appearance.   The Inspectorate's report on the
BEd in the colleges pleaded, for example, that education
studies, professional studies and school experience should be
more coherently built round a unifying thread of vocational
relevance. (18)   More generally, the anxiety behind pleas
for coherence has been that students would be allowed to
select whatever they wished from an open smorgasbord of
offerings, without regard to how the various items fitted
together, or rather failed to fit together.

These appeals for coherence are now also to be found in
discussions of the school curriculum.   For example, 'Aspects
of Secondary Education in England' advocated cutting down the
number of options and expanding the compulsory core as a way
of achieving greater coherence.   The report also warns us
that 'many schools were aware that a curriculum made up of
individual subjects, however carefully chosen to provide a
balanced programme, may not necessarily result in a coherent
experience for the pupils or provide all the opportunities that
they need.' (19)   This view is summed up in 'A View of the
Curriculum' when it says that 'there is need for more coherence within the experience of individual pupils.' (20)

The general meaning of 'coherence' seems clear enough.   It
is that of various elements fitting together according to some

principle.   Normally this fitting together is implied to be
something desirable, though that does not strictly follow:
egoism can be a coherent policy.   Coherent speech fits
together according to a thread of meaning, a coherent policy
has elements which complement and assist each other, while
the coherence theory of truth picks out as true those propositions which all fit together in a certain way (in what way is
unfortunately typically left unclear).

How would we fare in trying to respond to the instruction
'construct a coherent curriculum'?   As with balance - indeed
there are several striking parallels between the two as curricular principles - we should need some prior guidance on
certain important points.   But this time perhaps the first
question would not be about the elements that are involved
but about the principle on which the fitting together is to be
done.   Granted that principle, then we shall have an important determinant of the elements that are to be included, and
of course excluded too.

Upon what principle is coherence then to be sought?   It
may be that the principle involved is precisely that of providing a curriculum which has balance and breadth, behind which
notions will probably lurk some version of a liberal (or general) education.   Again, the principle involved may be a vocational one, as with the BEd comment mentioned earlier.   In
schools, the principle might be relevance to a specific career
or range of careers, though this is more common at the
further educational level.   The Further Education Review and
Development Unit suggested in their document 'A Basis for
Choice' that 'it can help to give coherence and a demonstrable
relevance to the various kinds of learning that occur in a
course if the whole can have some kind of focus - probably a
"vocational area or sector", if this term can be appropriately
defined.' (21)   With these alternative conceptions in mind one
can see that just as the same curricular programme could be
either balanced or unbalanced, so too could it be either coherent or incoherent, though from different points of view of
course.   As before, one is led to ask where the constraint
then lies in this principle.

The range of possible principles of coherence does not end
there.   Recall the view expressed earlier by the Inspectorate
that there is a need for more coherence within the experience
of individual pupils.   This suggests that although liberal and
vocational versions of the curriculum may achieve different
sorts of 'objective' coherence, the 'subjective' experience of
the pupil himself may be anything but coherent.   The device
of following a pupil through the course of a typical secondary
school day, with all its changes of classroom, teacher and
subject, has borne this thought in upon the minds of those
who have tried this experiment.

Balance and coherence

The upshot would seem to be that coherence, like balance, raises many more questions, and perhaps raises more important questions, than it answers.   It was for this reason that I said at the outset that the two principles were alike in being secondary.   Each can have a genuine function to perform in curricular debate, but neither can be regarded as fundamental.   They both assume an agreed framework of curricular and, still more broadly, of educational value-judgements.   If such a consensus exists, a debate in terms of them is probably pitched at the right level.   They may, however, serve precisely to conceal or to bypass the fact that a consensus does not exist, and then their function is primarily rhetorical.   In these respects, balance and coherence as curricular principles are from the same family as needs and relevance.   It may even have somewhere been earnestly said that while a balanced programme is what is needed, coherence is also relevant.   So far as my own observation goes, the prize for such vapidity must go to 'The School Curriculum', which blandly tells us that each pupil should have 'a broad programme, but one which includes what is essential and is coherent and balanced and properly suited to his needs'. (22) Nobody could possibly disagree with that, but then neither could anyone act on it.

IV

Many recent references to coherence, and especially to balance, have been made in the context of arguing against the provision of options towards the end of the secondary school course.   On this particular point, the DES and the Inspectorate appear to speak with one voice.   It has been argued, for example, that pupils' reasons for the options they choose are often rather bizarre and, more cogently, that early choosing may unwisely preclude later opportunities for employment or for continuing education.   Courses discontinued in the third year are said to be a waste of time through still earlier anticipation of dropping them and through truncation.   The arrangements made for options are said often to be of self-defeating complexity and often not to yield the options for which a preference has in fact been expressed.   And there have always been those who would argue for the benefits in terms of a liberal (or general) education of continuing to study a broad spectrum of varied subjects for as long as possible.

A progressively widening area of the compulsory is thus in consequence to be found in successive DES statements. 'Education in Schools' wanted a core consisting of English, mathematics, science, a modern language and of course religious education.   'A Framework for the Curriculum' added

physical education to that list, while 'The School Curriculum'
additionally though somewhat perfunctorily insisted on some
work from the humanities, a practical activity and an aesthetic
activity.

All of this adds up to quite a powerful case, but on the
other side there are many things to be said for an optional
element.   Not so very long ago, the Newsom Report on the
lower half of the secondary school ability range rested its
curricular case on four features: on being practical, realistic
and vocational, and also on incorporating choice.   'Freedom of
choice is something which all adolescents claim', we were
told. (23)   The requirement of subjective coherence mentioned earlier would also seem more likely to be met if the
pupil himself had had a say in what he is to study.   It has
been argued that if pupils are given some choice in what they
study, then they will study with more interest and effectiveness.   They will be able to build on their strengths and to
drop subjects in which they have displayed no aptitude.
They and their parents will be encouraged in taking a responsible attitude towards their futures.   Career intentions can
become operative, with a further motivational gain.   Since
the curriculum is itself a principal source of social control in
school, allowing a measure of choice makes control that much
easier than it would be with coerced and even resented study.
Pupils will already have achieved at least some degree of
'balance' by the time that they face these options and schooling is not the end of all opportunity in that respect anyway.
A compromise between balance and options is in any case to a
degree feasible through offering choices from within a range
of balanced groupings of subjects.   At sixth-form level, the
controversial characteristic of 'subject-mindedness' has been
mentioned to support not just options but specialisation by
'sides'. (24)

A fair-minded person confronted by these arguments might
well be perplexed as to which side has the better case.   He
might well conclude that here is a paradigm case of the need
for a compromise in which something is conceded to each of
two valid and important principles.   Why, then, have the
recent debates come down so decisively against options and in
favour of compulsion?   There appear to be two main sets of
considerations which explain this.

The first set of considerations is administrative.   With
rolls falling, numbers of teachers having to be reduced and
resources generally being cut back, options become that much
harder to staff and to finance.   Options produce small groups
in some subjects and require teachers from a wider range of
subjects.   In relation to considerations such as these, the
apparently educational principles of balance and coherence

have the function of putting a more attractive gloss on financial necessity and so conceal that something is being lost.   It
may well be that we do indeed have to bow to financial necessity here, but to what extent that is so will be a matter of
degree and it will not help in drawing the line if educational
loss is passed off as really being virtue.   One major risk
with such principles as balance and coherence, therefore, is
that they are so flexible that they can be made to bend to
any administrative breeze, while at the same time preserving
an appearance of being purely educational.

The second set of considerations running against options
appears to derive from the elusive matter of 'national need',
on which the Secretary of State claims a particular right of
superintendence.   What 'national need' amounts to is a set of
requirements stemming from the fact that our economy is part
of a competitive international network, that there is rapid
technological change and that we would do well to keep
abreast and if possible at the front of advances in microelec-
tronics.   We also need to give more attention to the formation of our engineers.   Thus 'The School Curriculum' affirms
in its second paragraph the apparently child-centred principle
of developing individual potential to the full.   In the following paragraph it defines that potential with reference to the
realities of adult life and, in the paragraph next after that,
adult life is defined in terms of a technology-based economy.

The document could scarcely have shown us more swiftly the
real concern of the DES in education, the impetus behind its
recent spate of documents and the explanation of its concentration on the later secondary school curriculum.   On the
other hand the Inspectorate's documents, while recognising
this economic theme to be a very important one, nevertheless
genuinely seek to retain something of an ampler and more
generous conception of education.   The ways in which these
tensions are reflected in differing versions of 'balance' are
interesting.   The Inspectorate's implicit conception of balance
is usually something rather Hirstian (though lacking Hirst's
rationale) with a physical and a linguistic dimension added.
By contrast, if we take something closer to the heart of
ministers, such as the Finniston Report 'Engineering Our
Future', then balance comes out as comprising mathematics,
physics, economics, English and a modern language. (25)
This is virtually identical to the DES's own 'Education in
Schools' (para. 2.13).

The first, financial set of considerations counting against
options shows balance being used to put an educational gloss
on financial necessity and thus to soothe any sense that educational damage is being done.   The second, technological set
of considerations shows balance being used to express a wish

for chips with everything, and for everyone.   What perhaps
mainly needs to be said on this second point is that it is a
fallacy, and also an educationally disastrous mistake, to infer
from the premise that society needs x the conclusion that
therefore everyone must learn x, whether 'x' is engineering
science, electronics or French.   Many pupils will face a
future of unemployment.   Many with employment will have no
need of technological expertise.   Some will certainly need the
technology which has so preoccupied the DES.   But it looks
very much like a species of overkill to impose a compulsory
'national need' version of balance on everyone, regardless of
ability and inclination, or more likely inability and disinclination.

REFERENCES

1   'A New Partnership for our Schools' (1977, HMSO).
2   See, for example, 'The School Curriculum' (1981, HMSO),
    para. 7.
3   'Education in Schools' (1977, HMSO).
4   'Primary Education in England' (1978, HMSO).
5   'Aspects of Secondary Education in England' (1979, HMSO).
6   'A Framework for the School Curriculum' (1980, HMSO).
7   Matters for Discussion 11:   'A View of the Curriculum'
    (1980, HMSO).
8   'The School Curriculum', op. cit.
9   'Education in Schools', op. cit., para. 1.19.
10   'A Framework for the Curriculum', op. cit., para. 9.
11   'The School Curriculum', op. cit., para. 11.
12   'Aspects of Secondary Education in England', op. cit.,
    ch. 3, para. 9.2.
13   Ibid., ch. 8, para. 14.5.
14   Schools Council Working Paper 55 (1975):   'The Curriculum
    in the Middle Years' (Evans/Methuen Educational), p. 27.
15   Schools Council Working Paper 53 (1975):   'The Whole
    Curriculum 13-16' (Evans/Methuen Educational), p. 46.
16   'Aspects of Secondary Education in England', op. cit.,
    ch. 3, para. 17.1.
17   'Education in Schools', op. cit., para. 2.13.
18   Matters for Discussion 8 (1979):   'Developments in the
    B.Ed. Degree Course' (1979, HMSO), pp. 46-7.
19   'Aspects of Secondary Education in England', op. cit.,
    ch. 9, para. 2.5.
20   'A View of the Curriculum', op. cit., p. 15, Proposition 5.
21   'A Basis for Choice' (1979, Further Education Curriculum
    Review and Development Unit), p. 8.
22   'The School Curriculum', op. cit., para. 14.
23   'Half Our Future' (1963, HMSO), para. 327.
24   'Subject-mindedness' was a psychological characteristic
    which the Crowther Report, '15 to 18' (1959), claimed was

a feature of those six per cent or so of sixth-form pupils
who were then intending to go to university.   It was
cited without evidence in the report as justifying specialisation exclusively on the science or the arts side of the
curriculum.   A.D.C. Peterson threw doubt on the whole
concept as a characteristic existing independently of institutional arrangements (see 'University Quarterly' for June
1960), but A. Beck argued that Peterson's empirical data
actually showed that a majority of such pupils would, in
ideal conditions, still favour specialisation on one side or
other (see 'Educational Review', 1972, vol. 24, no. 2).
25 'Engineering Our Future' (1980, HMSO), ch. 4.   This,
the Finniston Report, has been almost entirely neglected
by educationists, presumably because it was presented to
the Department of Industry and not to the DES.   But
chapter four especially contains much interesting educational material related to the 'formation' of engineers.

6 WHAT IS GENERAL ABOUT GENERAL EDUCATION?

Perhaps because it is thought to have an unacceptably elitist connotation, the term 'liberal education' seems to be dropping out of use - but the idea is certainly not dead. More usually, it finds currency under the neutral label of 'general education', although this classless newcomer is scarcely less ambiguous. 'General education' may simply connote an education for the generality of pupils as opposed to an education appropriate to some group thought to have special needs, such as the mentally defective or the markedly talented. More often the term picks out a programme which covers a full range of traditional subjects, as opposed to the specialised provision consequent upon a narrowing selection amongst options. Hard on the heels of general education in this second sense come the associated ideas of 'breadth' and 'balance'.

There is yet a third possible sense of 'general education' which has a long history and which shows every sign of renewed currency. This is the sense in which education is conceived as developing general powers of the mind, or abilities or skills which are not confined to particular subject divisions of the curriculum. Such mental abilities would, if they existed, have application across a whole range of subjects. To revive an earlier enthusiasm of psychological research, such abilities would rest on 'transfer of training'; but could there be such abilities? Could there be general powers of the mind?

This question has intermittently been part of the philosophical agenda during the past fifteen years, largely as a result of Professor Hirst's discussion of it in his now classic paper on liberal education. (1) Hirst returned an unhesitatingly negative answer to the question of such a possibility, and Professor Phillips Griffiths seemed to argue for the same conclusion. (2) However, R.K. Elliott subsequently raised a number of interesting points by way of counter-argument in an attempt to make the question at least an open one again. (3) There the matter seems largely to have rested. However, a number of recent statements, especially some statements contained in recent reports of Her Majesty's Inspectorate, make open-mindedness on this question a rather inadequate response to it. There is a need to consider once again whether there can be general powers of the mind.

What is general about general education?

Of course there is a sense in which generality attaches to
all learning.   Unless someone is able to recognise 'same again'
or is able to repeat a performance on another appropriate
occasion we would, barring special circumstances, decline to
say that he had learned.   A child has not learned to recognise the word 'field' unless he can identify it on other occasions, in other books and in capitals as well as in lower case.
Thus some generality attaches to all learning, but the argument over general powers of the mind is concerned with generality in a stronger sense than that.

Perhaps the classic historical expression of the existence of
general powers is to be found in Locke's 'Essay Concerning
Human Understanding'.   In his pursuit of the origin of all
our knowledge, Locke concluded that all of our ideas have
but two sources: sensation and reflection.   At first the
mind is as white paper, void of all characters, but then sensation gives us ideas of external objects and their properties.
Reflection gives us ideas of our own mental faculties, of which
there are two: volition and understanding.   Volition, or the
power to begin or forebear as we choose, will not concern us
further; but Locke's 'understanding' raises one important
aspect of our problem.   By 'understanding', he means to
embrace such more particular powers as perception, retention,
comparison, compounding, abstraction and judgement.   These
powers require sensory materials before they can begin to
operate, but they are regarded by Locke as being *original* in
the mind.   These original powers are then developed by suitable exercise. (4)

By the time of John Dewey, this idea had been developed
into a theory of the curriculum which Dewey called the 'theory
of formal discipline'. (5)   Each of the various curricular subjects was thought especially to be good for developing one or
other of the general mental powers.   Thus history was
thought to be good especially for the memory, science for
observation, mathematics for abstract reasoning, poetry for
imagination and classics for everything.   More recently, Glenn
Langford has aptly dubbed this theory the 'wall-bar theory of
the curriculum' on account of its implied view that mental
abilities are like muscles: you can strengthen them by exercise on some particular piece of apparatus but then they may
be employed on a much wider range of tasks. (6)

The chief observation that I would like to make about Locke's
conception is that the real or supposed originality of general
powers is beside the point.   Whether there can be general
powers of the mind is a question that can be considered independently of having to establish the nature of our mental
equipment in early infancy.   Let us suppose that someone
hostile to Locke succeeded in demonstrating that there could

be no such original general powers for the various subjects of
the curriculum then to develop by suitable exercises.   Still
it would not follow that general powers could not be an *outcome* of learning.   Nobody supposes children to be born with
an ability to play the piano, or to program computers, yet
such abilities can be acquired.   Why, then, might not still
more general abilities be acquired?   Admittedly something
would have to be presupposed as original.   As R.K. Elliott
has cogently argued, a wholly indefinite mind could never
develop any powers at all. (7)   For instance, no matter
what stimulating experiences you addressed to a tree, it
would never develop intelligence.   Children must bring something with them into the world, but it need not be general
powers of the kind that cut across whole ranges of curricular
subjects.

Locke's classical expression of the general powers thesis is
misleading also in a second way.   It gives the impression
today that the theory is tied to an outdated confusion between
psychology and epistemology, and so has only antiquarian
interest - but this is very far from being the case, and I
shall proceed to show that the theory is alive and well and is
to be found in some unexpected places.

So far as university education is concerned, Newman was
clearly an advocate of a general powers thesis.   He described
a cultivation of the intellect which was very far from being
confined to making scholarly acquaintance with certain subjects.   His aim was to cultivate 'a faculty of entering with
comparative ease into any subject of thought, and of taking
up with aptitude any science or profession'. (8)   As Hirst
has noticed, much the same idea persists in the Harvard
Report of 1946, 'General Education in a Free Society'.   That
report advocates seeking to develop general powers of the
mind which will enable us to think effectively, to make relevant judgements and to judge with discrimination. (9)   Again,
Professor Phillips Griffiths has identified a similar view in
P.H. Nowell-Smith's inaugural lecture of 1958, Education in a
University. (10)   Nowell-Smith saw it as the special task of
literature to develop creative imagination, of history to
develop practical wisdom and of philosophy to develop logical
thought.

As a final example of the supposed role of the university in
producing such 'generalists', we might take Wegener's recent
book 'Liberal Education and the Modern University'. (11)
Wegener declines to equate a liberal education with awareness
of any particular range of subjects or 'great thinkers'.   If
we were to specify some acquaintance with Shakespeare,
Newton, Darwin and Einstein as necessary, it would follow
that Plato could not have been educated liberally, and Wegener

understandably finds this an odd conclusion.   A liberal education, in Wegener's view, is to be found in the cultivation of
certain general powers of critical reflection which can then be
employed in many different specific directions.   This way of
looking at the matter, he thinks, is especially helpful if we
are perplexed by the vexing educational problem of proliferat-
ing university disciplines and the impossibility of making
acquaintance with them all.

However, it is not only university education that is conceived of in such terms.   The 1978 report of the Inspectorate, 'Primary Education in England', makes numerous references, especially in chapter five, to some supposed general
skills. (12)   The report attaches much importance to the
intellectual development of the more able and indeed average
pupils.   In part this needed shift in emphasis is envisaged
in terms of pursuing the usual curricular subjects in greater
depth.   That seems unexceptionable, but there is another
implicit conception of intellectual development as acquiring
certain general skills, and that seems more questionable.
Consider some of the examples given: learning to notice and
to think, learning to make sense of difficult passages, learning to make careful observations and acquiring a general
listening skill.   Could there be such general skills as these?

In the later booklet 'Mathematics 5-11' three justifications
are given for the teaching of mathematics.   First, there
comes the fully expected utilitarian argument and, second,
there is a reference to some more general cultural considerations; but it is the third justification which is of interest
here, namely that mathematics trains the mind. (13)   The
authors do not mean by this just that mathematics gives a
mathematical training, which would be unexceptionable enough.
They mean that some sort of more general training can result.
This is evident from the admission that other subjects might
also provide this general training, so that by itself this
feature could not be a justification specifically of mathematics.
They probably have in mind such familiar commonsense
assumptions as that mathematics trains us, quite generally, in
accuracy of statement or closeness of reasoning, but the same
claims have been made for other subjects too.

The impression that general powers of the mind are making
something of a comeback is further strengthened by a reading
of the recent official publication, 'A View of the Curriculum'.
In that document we can read that in the primary school 'skills
of observing, listening and touching need to be developed', (14) while in the secondary school 'engagement with
the processes of science should also be helping to strengthen
general powers of observation and reasoning.' (15)   Thus
although the theory may have had its origins in a classic

statement of Locke's, it would be quite wrong to think that it
was now only a historical curiosity, or that the generally
sceptical results of the psychological work on transfer of
training had put it to rest.   The theory is alive and well,
and can be found smiling at us from pages still warm from the
official press.

How is this resurgence in popularity to be explained?   Part
of the undoubted attraction has already been mentioned in
connection with Wegener's account of liberal education in a
modern university.   I refer to the proliferation of new disciplines, or the 'explosion in knowledge' as it has come to be
called.   General powers of the mind seem to offer a unifying
theme providing something common and sharable across the
various disciplines;   but an even grater attraction has been
the possibility of learning something of permanent value when
what counts as knowledge is apt to be subject to revision or
revaluation, and hence to be marred by obsolescence.

Examples of this obsolescence are easy to find.   The
teacher may tell his pupils of the igloos in which the Eskimos
live, when within a few years of his telling them this it is no
longer true that Eskimos live in igloos.   He may illustrate the
expansion of metals by reference to rail joints, when British
Rail are already pursuing a policy of continuous welding of
their track.   The Vikings are said to have had helmets with
horns, but then historians revise their ideas on that, and so
on.   Suppose that he could teach something that was less
vulnerable to change yet still of value?   If a teacher taught
that, then he could more reasonably hope that what his pupils
learned would continue to be of value to them long after they
had left school, or had changed their jobs for the third or
fourth time.   It is in this vein that Husén writes:

> ... in a changing society the school cannot provide an intel-
> lectual fare of specific items of knowledge for lifelong use.
> The shift that has to take place in the content of teaching
> is one from emphasis primarily on transmission of specific
> items of knowledge, which may soon become obsolete, to one
> with emphasis on the intellectual skills that are applicable to
> a broad - and largely unforeseen - repertoire of tasks and
> situations. (16)

The successful learner will become a man for all seasons.

A persuasive argument can be based on these desirable
features, but from the fact that something is desirable, even
very desirable, it by no means necessarily follows that it will
be possible.   What we would wish and what we might possibly
have quite regularly fail to coincide.   Many people would
apparently like immortality, but it by no means follows that a

pill or a medical procedure must be just round the corner to
secure this advantage.   Whether theological remedies are any
more certain I would not care to say.

An interjection which must next be considered is that the
problem of general abilities is a psychological problem.   As
such it should be left to the psychologists to sort out and is
no concern of philosophers at all.   One of the classic re-
searchers into this problem, E.L. Thorndike, defines the
problem as follows: 'The problem, which is clearly one of
psychological fact, may be best stated in psychological terms
as follows: How far does the training of any mental function
improve other mental functions?' (17)   Two experimental
approaches seem to have been adopted in research on transfer of training.   One approach is to see how far having
learned one thing facilitates the learning of another, for example how far having learned the piano facilitates learning to
type, or how far having learned something with the right hand
facilitates learning it with the left hand.   The other approach
is to measure attainment in various areas and then to see how
far there is a common factor which may then be identified as a
general ability.

It is possible, however, to proceed to empirical research too
quickly or too neglectfully of conceptual considerations.   For
example, research on dyslexia may be inconclusive precisely
because the concept of dyslexia is itself a source of ambiguity.
Is it just a descriptive term picking out specific reading disability as something that may be observed, or is it an explanatory concept implying some congenital deficiency or neurological abnormality, in which case evidence independent of the
observed reading disability ought to be produced?   Consider
sociological empirical research into poverty.   Does 'poverty'
imply the non-achievement of some absolute level of provision,
such as lack of the means to get such basic provisions as food
and shelter, or is it a relative concept, in which case only
having one car or a black-and-white television set might count
as poverty in some affluent society?   The extent of poverty
in a society cannot be determined independently of such conceptual variations.

Just as with dyslexia and poverty, so too with general abilities;   some thought should be given to conceptual considerations in conjunction with the carrying out of empirical research.   For consider, where there is correlation or facilita-
tion these things would be compatible with there being a general ability, but they might equally well be explained by the
presence of an interest or an attitude.   In 'Zen and the Art
of Motorcycle Maintenance', Pirsig suggested a certain Zen
state of peace of mind as a condition of general technical com-
petence (18) - but that is not an ability;   it is a condition in

which abilities may most profitably be exercised.   Consider a
pupil who does well in various map-reading skills: estimating
height and slope, calculating distances, giving directions,
following grid references, describing the problems a road
engineer would have to face and so on.   Someone who does
well at all of these tasks does not necessarily have a general
map-reading skill.   He may just be intensely interested in
anything to do with maps, and hence eagerly learns each
separate and specific task of map-reading.

On the other hand, where there is no correlation or facilita-
tion this is indeed compatible with the absence of any general
ability but it could equally well be explained as an educational
failure.   That is to say, the abilities we acquire are not
simply a function of the abilities that could be acquired but
are also a function of the teaching objectives in a given educational situation.   General abilities might have been possible,
but were never achieved because they were never made the
objective.   I was taught that $a^2-b^2 = (a+b)(a-b)$ without any
reference to the application of this to purely arithmetical problems, such as 17^2-13^2.   Presumably a test of my mathematical
abilities would have shown no transfer, yet transfer there certainly could have been.

Our present inquiry is therefore a conceptual one into the
possibility of general abilities or general powers of the mind,
although no doubt there could be many correlative empirical
inquiries which it would be appropriate to make.   Ideally the
evolution of an adequate view would involve interactive modification of concepts and data.   On the conceptual side, there
would seem to be no alternative in any particular case to some
form of content analysis, or reflection on the content of what
might be learned.   Indeed, Thorndike's own conclusion seems
to bear this out, for he says that 'only in so far as the two
functions have as factors identical elements' can there be facil-
itation (19) - but you discover whether there can be identical
elements in the first place by reflection on the possible content of what is to be learned.   Without such expectations,
you cannot interpret your own data.

Dealing with the interjection that the problem of general
abilities is a psychological problem, I therefore arrive at the
conclusion that in part, but only in part, this is so.   In part
also, however, it is a conceptual problem, and it is to some
conceptual aspects of the problem that I now turn.

One of the most cogent arguments on this question by a
philosopher in recent years has been that of Professor
Hirst. (20)   Hirst argues that any ability must be exercised
on something specific.   You cannot just attend, observe,
reason or imagine in a vacuum.   On the contrary, each of

those activities must be directed towards some specific object
or task.   Locke himself implicitly recognised this when he
said that his powers of the mind would first begin to operate
only when the mind was furnished by sensation with materials
on which to operate. (21)   Hirst continues by arguing that
the extent to which we may speak of an ability (rather than
an inability) will depend on our degree of success in observing, reasoning, imagining and so on; but what counts as
success will be *specific* to the subject-matter under consideration, or to the object or task with which we are engaged.
Therefore abilities must necessarily be specific and cannot be
general, since their public standards of success will be specific.   The able person may be a good mathematical problem-
solver, or a good botanical observer, or an imaginative historian, but he cannot be a good problem-solver in general, or a
good observer in general.   He may in fact be good in several
different areas, but in that case it will not be because he has
acquired a general ability but because he has a range of separate abilities.   If this is so, then we should scarcely be surprised to find, as Dewey observes, that a highly trained
authority in one field may be a very poor judge in another.

Professor Phillips Griffiths has a similar although more briefly argued point to make. (22)   Griffiths argues that mentalistic concepts such as 'intelligent' or 'imaginative' need to be
schematised.   (Presumably the reference is to Kant's doctrine
that very general categorial concepts like causality require
something intermediate for their application to particular instances.)   Griffiths argues that such concepts must be
'given a concrete sense in terms of some particular activity'
and are indeed best understood adverbially.   The force of
the adverbs 'intelligently' or 'imaginatively' will depend on
what they qualify.   The result is the same as with Hirst:
being an imaginative scientist is concluded to be a very different thing from being an imaginative poet.

My comment on this line of argument is that part of its conclusion seems undeniable.   The successful exercise of an
ability will indeed require reference to specific criteria of
success, to which we may add specific knowledge of various
kinds - but it does not follow that there can be nothing
general.   Consider the case of seeing.   To see the reed
warbler, or the constellation of Orion, or the symptoms of
pneumonia, will require specific abilities and knowledge, but
there can still be something general present in all the variety
of cases, even if it is only the general power of focusing our
visual attention.   Educationally, that example is not very
exciting: we would either have such a power or not have it,
without much room for educational improvement; but if the
example is sufficient to show general powers to be possible,
we could proceed to see if there might be some educationally
more interesting ones.

Before doing that, however, R.K. Elliott's argument in
favour of general powers of the mind must be considered.
Elliott's chief argument appears to be that there are criteria
of sameness which identify unitary abilities exercised on a
variety of subject-matters.   On reflection, it might be
thought odd if this were not so.   After all, we use the same
term in each case, although Wittgensteinian points about family
resemblance might also be pertinent here.   An example which
Elliott chooses is that of understanding. (23)   On a Hirst-
Griffiths view, there could be no general power of understanding.   On the contrary, there could only be an understanding of French or of physics or of people's motivation,
and so on.   However, Elliott argues that whether we are to
understand the French Revolution or Wittgenstein's philosophy
or Hamlet or Dartmoor, if our understanding is to be a fully
developed or excellent one then it will in every case exhibit
these same features: truth, comprehensiveness, profundity,
and a grasp which is synoptic, critical, firm, sensitive to the
less obvious features, fertile and justly appreciative.   Thus
understanding is a general power of the mind.

My own comment on this argument is that it confuses conditions for the application of a concept with the presence of a
unitary psychological ability.   For example, there may indeed
be features common to all skilled performances in virtue of
which we call them all skilled, but it does not follow that it is
the same skill which is present in each case: in the skater,
the juggler, the flautist, the chess player and the linguist.
Take the case of judgement.   Certainly there is something
common to all instances of what we call good judgement.
This may arguably be said to be getting something right in
difficult circumstances, but it is very different and specific
accomplishments which are necessary to get things right in
difficult circumstances.   The judgement of the politician, the
cricket player, the car driver, the investor and the pilot are
very different things, and we should be very unwise to
assume that an excellent wicket keeper would therefore be
just the man to exercise political judgement in a damaging
strike.   As Aristotle argued against Plato, there is no single
good present in all cases, but many different goods resting
on different bodies of knowledge: the good general is not
possessed of the same abilities as the good doctor, and he is
different again from the good gymnast.

However, even if Elliott's argument fails in its objective of
re-establishing the possibility of general powers of the mind,
that does not imply that such powers are impossible.   It
means only that he has given us no reason to think that they
are possible.   The earlier example of the focusing of visual
attention in seeing was claimed to establish at least the possibility, even if in an educationally rather uninteresting case.

What is general about general education?

I would like now to return to the earlier point that the first
step in an inquiry into general abilities ought to be to reflect
on the possible learning content.   It was suggested that this
reflection must precede empirical investigation, otherwise it
would not be possible to interpret the data collected.   In reflecting on possible content, a broad distinction needs first to
be made between general ideas and general skills.   By
'general ideas' I mean ideas with a broad range of applications
but having their origin in a single subject or discipline.   For
example, someone may know how to lever off the lid of a tin,
but if he knew the principles of leverage including the various classes of lever he would have a more general idea, in
this case drawn from mechanics.   Again, someone may know
that 5+3 = 3+5, but he has a more general idea if he knows
that it is a law of arithmetic that a+b = b+a.   Furthermore,
a West European who knows the shape of the earth has a more
general idea than one who knows the shape of Taiwan, since
the known shape of the earth will have a vastly greater range
of applications in organising his experience.   Looking back to
our opening remarks on the kinds of general education, yet
another kind might now be noted, namely an education concerned more with general ideas than with ideas of very limited
application.

Can there, by contrast, be general skills which are not tied
in origin to a particular subject or discipline?   A controversial example of this possibility is general intelligence, understood not in some technical and operationally defined sense of
the psychologist but in its everyday sense as quickness of
learning.   Someone might surely generally be intelligent in
the sense that he is quicker than others quite generally at
learning.   He gets the point, sees what is at issue, spots
the relevant pattern or relation and masters a wide variety of
tasks faster than do others.   It seems to me to be an evident
fact of daily experience that there are such differences of
general learning ability, and this fact must be even more
obvious to a teacher who is constantly in the position of setting learning tasks to varied groups of people.   What is much
more obscure is what the content of such an ability might be.
What is it that the intelligent person knows?   Is it not so
much something that he knows as a neurological or biochemical
difference?   In the latter case, intelligence would be a matter
of 'native wit', implying that there is not much that formal
education could do to alter it (except possibly to call in the
teacher at conception).

It still remains to find an example of an ability which is
general, teachable and educationally interesting, and I suggest
that such an ability is possible in relation to problem-solving.
It is possible to describe, or rather to prescribe, a set of
rules or tactics which someone might learn and which would be

relevant to solving a very wide range of problems not confined to a single subject or discipline.   A person with general
problem-solving ability might have learned how to deploy the
following rules or tactics with skill: pick out essentials;   dis-
criminate between what is relevant and what is irrelevant;
identify assumptions and consider their acceptability;   look
for analogous problems the solution to which is already known;
refrain from being critical of emerging suggestions too early;
try a different way of looking at the problem, or redefine it
in a different way.

Consider this last injunction: to redefine the problem in a
different way.   A teacher may define his school's problem as
one of providing sufficiently for pastoral care, but it may be
better to redefine the problem as one of providing a more
appropriate curriculum, which would eliminate one-half of the
'pastoral' problems which seem so to oppress.   Take an example of de Bono's: in a narrow, walled country lane, how is
an ambulance to get past a flock of sheep?   There seems to
be no way, since sheep cannot be persuaded to squeeze to
one side - but if the problem is redefined as one of getting
the sheep past the ambulance, possible solutions come into
view.   Again, Edward Jenner was led to his discovery of
vaccination against smallpox by redefining the problem of why
people get smallpox in other terms as the problem of why
other people do not get smallpox.   So we have three examples
of problems from very different fields to all of which a general
strategy has a useful contribution to make.   Such contributions are possible right across the range of Hirst's 'forms of
knowledge'.   Something of the above idea is behind the
advocacy of 'learning how to learn', although this kind of
learning is rarely further analysed. (24)

I have argued that there is nothing conceptually impossible
about a general power of the mind.   I have done this first by
separating the issue from Lockian speculations about the equipment originally supplied to us in infancy, then by showing how
it is not just an empirical psychological problem, and next by
meeting Hirst's arguments but without reliance on a defective
argument of Elliott's.   Finally, I have sought to clinch the
matter by producing an example of a possible general ability
which is both teachable and educationally interesting.   I
should now hasten to add that I am not suggesting that such
a general ability would ever be sufficient, or that it would be
the only thing of educational value to emerge from a particular
learning task.

Clearly the general features in problem-solving ability could
not be sufficient, for the reasons which Hirst gives.   Specific criteria and specific knowledge are necessary too.   A
graduate generalist still needs specific job training before he

What is general about general education?

is of much use to his employer.   Even if he had some general
problem-solving ability he would still need to learn specific
rules, the resources available, and the characteristics of his
fellow workers before he began to produce realistic problem
solutions.   It was observed when creativity tests were the
fashion, typified by the question concerning the uses of a
brick, that the 'uses' which would occur to people depended
in part on what they knew about bricks.   For example, would
it be a creative 'solution' to suggest that bricks might be used
to make a boat?   My suggestion, therefore, is not that general abilities are sufficient for some task, but that they are
possible and being possible they might have valuable contributions to make.   Hirst's argument shows specifics to be necessary but does not show something general to be impossible.

In so far as a general ability might begin to emerge from a
particular learning task, for example if this is made one objective in teaching, that would not mean that this would be the
only thing of educational value to emerge.   Presumably the
point of general abilities lies precisely in their specific applications and is therefore instrumental only.   Herein lies the
mistake of those defenders of classics in the schools who
argue that classics gives a general mental training.   For the
sake of argument, let us suppose that it does do this.   Other
subjects might do it too, so that a specific justification of
classics has not been given;   and the other subjects might
additionally have a specific value, so that there is a double
value in them.   If classics is defensible, it would need to be
defended more amply than this.

Does all this mean that the currently growing popularity of
the idea of general skills or abilities is justified?   There do
seem to be some possibilities worth investigating and making
into teaching objectives - but other examples seem to rest on
features of generality which are educationally trivial, and
hence it would be misdirected effort to emphasise them.   I
have in mind particularly some of the 'general skills' referred
to earlier in the Inspectorate's report 'Primary Education in
England'.   That report for the most part assumes a very
acceptable conception of intellectual development as pursuing
the usual curricular subjects in greater depth.   However,
especially in chapter five, the report seems to assume the
existence and value of some rather more dubious general
skills, such as observation and listening.

Take the case of observation.   Observation follows specific
interest and knowledge, without which we just do not see the
bond used in the brick wall, the fine structure of the feather,
the cue-mark in the corner of the television picture or the
subtle change in someone's mood.   Being generally observant
seems even to be self-contradictory, since to be observant is

to be attentive to some specific but easily missed feature in a
scene which is always infinite in its variety of possible descriptions.   If there is anything common at all to all cases of
being observant, it is probably just our general power of
focusing attention, although there might be a readiness to find
features of unexpected interest in the environment as a more
valuable general attitudinal outcome.   Typically, however,
when children are said to be observant there is some specific
context which the speaker has in mind, such as scientific ex-
perimentation or, even more particularly, a single but memorable instance of a child's surprising remark upon noticing
something.

General listening skill does not seem to stand in much better
case.   If you are to pick out the robin, the need for tappet
adjustment, the key change in the music, the Frenchman's
message or the touch of envy in the voice, you need specific
interests and knowledge.   Again, all that is general appears
to be auditory attention.   When teachers say that children
today do not listen, they normally mean not that some general
skill is being neglected but that, for example, having television on all the time at home has produced a habitual disregard
for what is said to them.

Could there be general powers of the mind?   Yes, there
could be and perhaps there already are, but not all of them
would be educationally interesting.   We would have to proceed in each case first by reflection on the possible learning
content of such a skill or ability.   Then empirical investigation would be appropriate into the effectiveness of different
teaching strategies in realising such a possible teaching objective.   No doubt this empirical work would occasionally lead us
to think again about the originally supposed possibility and its
content, as well as about the kind of teaching which is most
facilitatory.   As to which the profitable examples might be,
it would seem best to consider them case by case.

REFERENCES

1 Hirst, P.H. (1965), Liberal education and the nature of
   knowledge, in Archambault, R.D. (ed.), 'Philosophical
   Analysis and Education' (London, Routledge & Kegan Paul).
2 Griffiths, A. Phillips (1965), A deduction of universities,
   in Archambault, op. cit.
3 Elliott, R.K. (1975), Education and human being, in
   Brown, S.C. (ed.), 'Philosophers Discuss Education'
   (London, Macmillan).
4 Locke, J. (1690), 'Essay Concerning Human Understanding', bk 2, ch. 1, section 20.
5 Dewey, J. (1916), 'Democracy and Education' (London,
   Macmillan), ch. 5, section 3.

6 Brown, S.C. (ed.) (1975), 'Philosophers Discuss Education', op. cit., p. 74.
7 Ibid., p. 54.
8 Newman, J.H. (1853), 'The Idea of a University', preface.
9 Hirst, P.H. (1965), in Archambault, op. cit., p. 116ff.
10 Griffiths, A. Phillips (1965), in Archambault, op. cit.,
   pp. 202-5.
11 Wegener, C. (1978), 'Liberal Education and the Modern
   University' (University of Chicago).
12 Department of Education and Science (1978), 'Primary
   Education in England' (London, HMSO).
13 Department of Education and Science (1979), 'Mathematics
   5-11' (London, HMSO), pp. 4-5.
14 Department of Education and Science (1980), 'A View of
   the Curriculum' (London, HMSO), p. 11.
15 Ibid., p. 16.
16 Husen, T. (1979), 'The School in Question' (Oxford University Press), p. 153.
17 Grose, R.F. and Birney, R.C. (eds) (1963), 'Transfer of
   Learning' (New York, van Nostrand), pp. 1-2.
18 Pirsig, R.M. (1974), 'Zen and the Art of Motorcycle Maintenance' (London, Bodley Head), ch. 25.
19 Grose, R.F. and Birney, R.C. (eds) (1963), op. cit., p.
   2.
20 Hirst, P.H. (1965), in Archambault, op. cit., pp. 116-21.
21 Locke, J. (1690), op. cit., bk 2, ch. 1, section 23.
22 Griffiths, A. Phillips (1965), op. cit., p. 203.
23 Elliott, R.K. (1975), op. cit., pp. 46-9.
24 A brief analysis of 'learning how to learn' can be found in
   Dearden, R.F. (1976), 'Problems in Primary Education'
   (London, Routledge & Kegan Paul), ch. 6.

7 CONTROVERSIAL ISSUES AND THE CURRICULUM

If by 'logical positivism' is meant that particular kind of hard-headedness presented by A.J. Ayer in his philosophical classic 'Language, Truth and Logic', then it seems to be very much in decline in academic philosophy. But it often happens that a philosophical position is a critical elaboration of an attitude or outlook which is abundantly present in a less examined way at the level of commonsense, or for that matter in non-philosophical educational theorising. For example, much that is of a positivist spirit is to be found in behaviourism and its offspring, such as the behavioural objectives movement and certain calls for more objective styles of assessment, and more generally in strong attachment to the observable and quantifiable as our sole guiding light.

If a curriculum were to be based on the principles of logical positivism, whether knowingly or unknowingly, it would presumably have to avoid those subject areas designated by Ayer as 'nonsense'. The nature of 'nonsense' here was determined by what is excluded from a classification of significant propositions into two broad categories: those which are analytic and *a priori* and those which are synthetic and empirical. That is very roughly to say that significant propositions must either be known from a consideration of the meanings of terms (perhaps mathematics and certain aspects of language) or else known by reference to sense-experience (for example, science and geography). Any other seemingly propositional area would be designated as 'nonsense' (I pass over the possible confusion between meaning and truth here). Thus 'nonsense' would embrace much that in the normal school curriculum is included under such subject headings as moral or social education, political education, religious education and literature and the arts. Such studies should largely disappear if the curriculum were henceforth to concern itself solely with knowledge, positivistically defined, as opposed to what would be seen as the non-cognitive social conditioning of attitudes or the mere expression of emotions.

Such an approach to deciding the content of the curriculum might be thought to exclude all reference to *controversial* matters, and many people who have given thought to the curriculum as a whole have felt that this brisk and brusque dismissal of the controversial on the grounds that it was not

'knowledge' was unwarranted.   I want to argue in this paper
that their intuitive reluctance would be right: the controversial is not simply an epistemological disaster area into which
the responsible curriculum constructor should not care to go.

   Accordingly, I propose to examine more closely the notion of
the controversial and then to see what implications that examination might have for the curriculum.   This is, of course,
not the same thing as to examine logical positivism itself.   A
project of such large scope is not my intention.   I shall
here confine myself to a consideration of one consequence of
its application to the design of curricula.

An immediate difficulty that has to be faced is that what is
meant by 'controversial' may itself be a matter of controversy.
For example, it is evident that some writers have adopted a
behavioural criterion of the controversial.   Charles Bailey
writes: 'that an issue is controversial is, of course, a matter
of social fact.   That is, an issue is controversial if numbers
of people are observed to disagree about statements and assertions made in connection with the issue.' (1)   But is it really
so obvious that this behavioural criterion is the most appropriate one to adopt?   I shall argue that the adoption of such a
criterion has at least two unfortunate consequences.

   In the first place, much of the disagreement which socially
occurs reflects either simple ignorance or else mere undisciplined assertiveness.   Children will dispute endlessly about
the capital cities of countries, spellings of words, authors of
books and explanations of well-understood natural phenomena,
yet in each case there exists a clear decision-procedure and
typically there is also a publicly known and available answer.
These matters are not controversial at all.   The answers are
definitely known.   What is controversial cannot, therefore, be
a simple 'matter of social fact'.

   In the second place, Bailey's criterion could give undeserved
encouragement to relativism (quite contrary to his own declared
sympathies, it must be said).   If all that is needed is for a
number of people to assert a counter-opinion for the matter to
become controversial, regardless of that counter-assertion's
ungroundedness, inconsistency, invalidity or mere expressive-
ness of a vested interest, then even the shape of the earth
becomes at once controversial.   Some say, and many more in
the past have said, that its shape is flat.   That is a matter
of social fact.   But what have such social facts got to do with
the shape of the earth?   This planet goes imperturbably on
its way regardless of our utterances, and its shape can be
known by anyone concerned seriously to find out.   The
behavioural criterion of the controversial therefore encourages

the thought that what is true should be collapsed into what
some group regards as true, with epidemic relativism and a
sociological carnival as the result.

What I suggest, by contrast, is an *epistemic* criterion of
the controversial.   Such a criterion might be formulated
somewhat as follows: a matter is controversial if contrary
views can be held on it without those views being contrary to
reason.   By 'reason' here is not meant something timeless
and unhistorical but the body of public knowledge, criteria of
truth, critical standards and verification procedures which at
any given time has been so far developed.   It follows that
what at one time is controversial may later be definitely
settled, as with many opinions about the nature of the surface of the moon and the character of the side that faces
away from the earth.   At one time these were matters of legitimate dispute in a way which at least some of them no longer
are.

By way of further illustration, several possible kinds of
controversial issue may be distinguished.   First, there are
those cases where we simply have insufficient evidence to
settle the matter, though in principle there is no reason why
it should not be settled as more or better evidence becomes
available.   Thus at a particular juncture the government of
the day may create mortgage controls in order to slow down
the rise in house prices.   Will the measure have the desired
effect?   That is controversial;   some evidence both for and
against its likely effectiveness is available.

A second type of case is where consideration-making criteria
are agreed but the weight to be given to them is not.   Thus
we all will agree that in considering whether the Vale of Bel-
voir should have its underground coal resources exploited
both environmental and economic criteria are relevant.   But
presumably local residents and the National Coal Board weight
these consideration-making criteria rather differently.   The
matter is controversial, and probably more intractably so than
in the first type of case.

A third and still more intractable case may be found where
there is no agreement even on the criteria as to what will
count.   In considering the admissibility of torture to obtain
information from prisoners, some will assume a consequentialist
criterion and so pick out resultant benefit and harm as what
should settle the matter.   Others will take a more intrinsica-
list view and argue that torture by its very nature, and quite
apart from its consequences, has a certain inherent moral
character.   To take another case, in the assessing of essays
the disputes which arise between markers may well be of this
third type, as when accuracy is prized by one and imaginative

expression by another (disputes about assessment may also be of types one or two, of course).

There is still a fourth possible case.   This is where not just individual criteria but whole frameworks of understanding are different.   Suppose that a person feels somewhat depressed, as many of us from time-to-time are apt to do.   Should that depression be regarded from a medical perspective as something calling for treatment, perhaps the prescription of some pills, or should it be regarded from an ethical perspective as something calling for a display of patience, fortitude, courage or endurance?   If that seems to be an unreal contrast, try reading Illich's critique of the medical profession, especially the American medical profession. (2)   To take an educational case, consider the differences of possible approach that might be adopted towards pupil behaviour that is perceived as undesirable.   Should we look at it most appropriately as in need of reshaping by the techniques of behaviour modification; or as in need of investigation in terms of psychoanalytic causes; or as in need of interpreting along the lines of a Marxist social analysis making reference to alienation and class domination; or more simply as expressive of an unsuitable choice of curricular material or staff attitudes along the lines that Rutter (3) has investigated - or just as perverse?   The matter is controversial.   A final example of this fourth type of controversy would be the controversy between the religious believer and non-believer over the correct description of a great many things in the world.

We now have before us both a suggested epistemic criterion of the controversial ('contrary views can be held without those views being contrary to reason') and an illustrative range of types of controversial issue.   But before proceeding to draw some educational implications, I would like to make certain general comments on the type of subject matter that may be controversial.   For it seems often to be assumed, and not least by those of positivist sympathies with whom we began, that it is especially matters of *value* which are controversial. Lawrence Stenhouse was apparently of this opinion when he wrote 'by a controversial issue we mean one which divides students, parents and teachers because it involves an element of value-judgement which prevents the issue's being settled by evidence and experiment'. (4)   Stenhouse's difficulty is at least epistemological and not just social, but there is a strong hint of positivist assumptions here.

But this confinement of the controversial to matters of value is a misconception.   Many empirically factual matters can also be controversial, so that having to do with values is by no means a necessary condition.   Why did the dinosaurs die out? How is one to explain what look like water-courses on Mars?

These are matters of scientific controversy.   Even mathematics
is not exempt.   Is every even number the sum of two primes?
Can n be any whole number greater than 2 in the equation
$x^n + y^n = z^n$?   These are controversial mathematical issues.

Having to do with values is not even a sufficient condition
for being controversial, let alone a necessary condition.
There are value-judgements which are entirely uncontroversial.
Consider for example the entirely uncontroversial aesthetic
value-judgement that Turner was a vastly superior painter to
myself (and probably yourself too).   Consider the moral
value-judgement that it is not only wrong but viciously so
when someone amuses himself by stubbing out burning cigar-
ettes on a baby entrusted to his care (I draw my example
from life).

What can be said about the predilection for citing value
matters as examples of the controversial is probably this.
The justification of value-judgements is, at least at certain
points, importantly different from the grounding of scientific
or mathematical assertions.   You could not ultimately settle
the moral character of baby-burning by appeal solely to scientific (and still less to mathematical) reasoning.   And the
ways in which value-judgements are different may make it
more likely that they will prove controversial.   But this is
not to say either that all, or that only, value-judgements are
controversial.   And let us also note that even the most tightly controlled of scientific enquiries is itself shot through with
values.   Why has the inquirer chosen that problem?   What of
the social consequences of the discovery he is about to make
and the resources used in making it?   Does not the very process of inquiry itself embody important virtues constitutive of
what we might call the 'ethics of belief' (you ought not to rush
to conclusions, you ought to be patient with difficulties, do
justice to objections, submit your work to criticism, etc. etc.)?
The logical positivist himself is presumably prescribing to us
what he regards, however misconceivedly, as a proper sense
of responsibility about our epistemic claims.   If values are
dirty, his own hands are far from clean.

By way of final general comment on the type of subject
matter that may be controversial, let us note that being controversial is no reason to cease from trying to settle a matter.
I suggested earlier that all kinds of historical contingencies
affect what at any given time is properly to be regarded as
controversial.   A matter which is in principle capable of
definite settlement will only come to be definitely settled if we
do not cease from trying to settle it.   And where value-
judgements are concerned, as Nordenbo (5) observes, to
regard them as being controversial at least assumes a cognitive theory of ethics.   What is controversial is precisely the

truth, correctness or rightness of some view, which presupposes that at least it makes sense to search for these things
even if we do not attain them.   Without that presupposition,
there is nothing controversial but just different personal pref-
erences, susceptible of explanation perhaps, but not appropriately open to calls for further justification or the citing of
evidence.

Is it educationally desirable that controversial issues should be
included in the curriculum?   One implication of the previous
argument is that this question cannot be answered in terms of
a division between controversial and uncontroversial *subjects*,
since all subjects have both controversial and uncontroversial
areas in them.   The simple positivist division between science
and mathematics, for example, and social, moral, political,
religious and aesthetic values is not just simple but simplistic.
The division between the controversial and the uncontroversial
cuts right across such a subject division, though no doubt the
extent of what is definitely settled as against what is more
open to the holding of contrary views will vary in different
subjects.

Granted that much, the question may still be raised whether
the controversial in each subject should, provided that its
level of difficulty or presupposed maturity are appropriate, be
tackled as part of the curriculum.   There are at least two
good reasons why it should be tackled.   The first reason is
given by Lawrence Stenhouse.   In spite of Stenhouse's well-
known attachment to the principle of 'procedural neutrality'
he certainly was not neutral towards the inclusion of controversial issues.   Where these concern matters of 'widespread
and enduring significance' he thinks that an education which
ignored them would be seriously inadequate.   And I agree
with him.   If, for example, the relationships between men and
women, or the principles according to which benefits and bur-
dens are distributed in a society, or family relationships, or
attitudes towards work, or the proper uses to be made of our
knowledge, or how we live, are never given any attention in
the course of our education, then matters of very great importance will have been neglected and opportunities for developing
a better informed, more sensitive, more discriminating and in
general more adequate understanding of these matters will
have been missed, perhaps even in some cases irrevocably.
But much to do with these matters is indeed controversial.

The second reason for including the controversial is not un-
related to the first.   It is just that to teach a subject in a
way that makes no reference to the controversial parts of it is
to misrepresent it.   This misrepresentation may arise simply
through giving the impression that a subject is a monolithic

block of certain knowledge which requires only that we turn
to the appropriate authority in order for any problem concerning it to be solved.   In this way the truth-criteria,
critical standards and verification procedures appropriate to
the subject may never themselves be mentioned.   If, however,
controversial matters are raised, then immediately there is an
open invitation explicitly to consider how they might be
settled.

But this is still not enough.   Ignoring the controversial
further misrepresents the subject in its nature as a historically developed line of inquiry.   The slightest acquaintance
with this historical dimension would reveal that progress has
been very far from smooth and automatic.   The history of
science, for example, is littered with the wreckage of successfully contested theories.   At the cutting-edge of any subject,
much, if not everything, will be controversial and if that cutting-edge is at present too remote from anything that could
be grasped by pupils at school, this is not so if we look to
the past of the subject.   Even something so uncontroversial
now as the function of the heart and the circulation of the
blood was at first hotly contested.   And it is not an idle
luxury to appreciate this.   It is essential to an adequate
grasp of the nature of human inquiry, of its dependence on
imaginative ideas, of the place of criticism in it, of its advancement sometimes by fruitful wrong ideas rather than by pedestrian right ones, and of its tools and standards.

How should the controversial be tackled?   Stenhouse's
answer was in terms of 'procedural neutrality'.   According to
this principle, which has undergone modifications and restate-
ments, the teacher should not indicate his own preferred solution or loyalty.   On that he should preserve a silence (though
much besides the mouth may speak).   Indeed, he should 'protect divergence', or encourage a full range of diverse views.
But his role is not to be otherwise passive.   On the contrary,
he should seek 'improved understanding' by a process of feed-
ing into the discussion or inquiry 'rich, diverse and balanced
evidence'.   Reactions to these procedural proposals have
varied from incomprehension, through doubt as to their desirability, to denial of their possibility.

It is in fact quite possible to be epistemically neutral on
some matter, for example acupuncture.   This may seem not to
be so if we are faced with the dilemma that, regarding any
particular candidate for belief, we must either believe it or not
believe it, from which the conclusion is drawn that we cannot
be neutral.   However, 'not believing' is not necessarily dis-
believing.   We may have no view about it at all, or never have
considered it.   Smith must either believe in acupuncture or
not believe in it.   If we suppose him not to believe in it,

this does not necessarily mean he disbelieves in acupuncture:
he may be either completely ignorant of this medical practice,
or he may be aware of its existence but have formed no view
on it at all.   Therefore epistemic neutrality on some matters
is quite possible.

But is such neutrality possible for a *teacher* of the matter
in question?   One cannot teach without framing intentions
about what is to be learnt and about how it is to be learnt.
And it will not be possible to frame such intentions without
some definite, even if provisional, view on the epistemic
status of what is taught.   Does the teacher intend it to be
realised that the view is definitely true or false, correct or
mistaken, right or wrong - or controversial?   Whatever the
answer here, including the answer that the view is to be seen
as controversial, there is a definite epistemic commitment.   It
is as much an epistemic commitment to regard the existence of
God as controversial as it is to regard it as known to be
either true or false.   Furthermore, in general the teacher
is, or if he is not then he ought to be, better able than his
pupils to assess the various views and claims that are made in
his curriculum area.   Where his judgement is that a matter is
both controversial and important enough to teach, then a
realisation on the part of the pupils of that controversiality
will be precisely one of his teaching objectives.   And the
teaching procedures which he should adopt will follow from
that.

Much that was puzzling in Stenhouse's approach can now be
made clearer, or perhaps corrected.   'Improved understanding' will, amongst other things no doubt, imply an appreciation of the controversial nature of the matter in hand, which
may of course involve moving the pupil away from inadequate-
ly based certainties.   'Protecting divergence' may be the
appropriate way of disclosing this controversiality, but merely
ignorant alternatives or mere undisciplined assertiveness imply
a behavioural and not an epistemic criterion of the controversial.   And the teacher may confront such massive prejudice
that *he* is the only source of possible 'divergence' - in which
case he can scarcely retain 'procedural neutrality'.   Again,
what 'evidence' should he supply, when should he introduce
it, with what force or insistence, how often should he recall
it and when is it 'balanced'?   No progress can be made in
answering such necessary questions until the epistemic objective is determined: seeing the matter as true, or as false, or
perhaps as controversial.

If this is right, then it is to pitch camp in the wrong place
to insist on 'procedural neutrality' as a principle.   It is just
a technique, not a principle, and one which is sometimes useful and sometimes not.   There are many other techniques of

teaching the controversial: stating both sides of the question, getting committed and even enthusiastic one-sided statements which are contextually understood to be one-sided, putting the missing side oneself, practising role-reversal (for example stating the opposite to one's own view oneself), debates, simulation games, framing alternative hypotheses, and so on.

Granted that the context is an educational one, and not one in which indoctrination is sought, then the corresponding dangers are fairly clear: covertly biased presentation, catechetical questioning seeking to establish a contentious orthodoxy, systematic institutional reinforcement of just one view, and the like.   The usual examples illustrative of these dangers are religious, as when the Plowden Report (paragraph 572) asserted that pupils 'should not be confused by being taught to doubt before faith is established'.   But we might equally turn to politics for examples.   A 1978 national college-entrance examination in China contained the following obviously catechetical questions: 'Why must countries having a dictatorship of the proletariat practice democracy towards the people and impose dictatorship on the enemy?   Criticise the Gang of Four's counter-revolutionary crimes of reversing the relations between the enemy and ourselves and imposing a fascist dictatorship on the people'. (6)   But although this illiberal way of treating what are really controversial issues is most obviously to be found in such areas as the religious and the political, it may exist wherever a matter is epistemically controversial, for instance in science, geography, history, or for that matter in educational theory.   Consider the often naive faith exhibited by those who preface their claims by saying, with innocent confidence, 'research shows'.   This, too, can be a result of teaching.

A final perplexity deserves mention.   I have assumed throughout this discussion that there will be a concurrence of judgement, at least amongst serious inquirers if not amongst the ignorant or merely assertive, as to what *is* controversial. But suppose that that assumption is false.   Suppose that there is no agreement as between a biology and a religious education teacher over the evolution of species, the one regarding it as a known historical fact while the other regards it as, if not definitely false, then at least controversial.   To take another example, consider the arguments against letting Stenhouse go ahead with the publication of his pack on race relations as a controversial issue.   One such argument put forward was that race relations are not a controversial issue for anyone who regards them with moral seriousness.

The point here is that serious and mature people can be in disagreement precisely over what is controversial, in the epistemic sense.   One party regards the matter as definitely

known while the other regards it as controversial.   Can there
be a rational solution in such cases?   Does it just depend on
who is finally in a position to enforce his view?   Should it,
or more pertinently could it, be settled by some such demo-
cratic procedure as voting (see Phillips (7))?   Should the
step be taken of calling in 'experts' to pronounce, in which
case what would be the character of their expertise?   Perhaps it is fortunate that concerning much that is controversial, it is at least uncontroversial that it *is* controversial.

REFERENCES

1 Bailey, C. (1975), Neutrality and Rationality in Teaching,
   in Bridges, D. and Scrimshaw, P. (eds), 'Values and
   Authority in Schools' (London, Hodder & Stoughton), p.
   122.
2 Illich, I. (1977), 'Limits to Medicine' (Harmondsworth,
   Penguin).
3 Rutter, M. et al. (1979), 'Fifteen Thousand Hours'
   (London, Open Books).
4 Schools Council/Nuffield Foundation (1970), 'The Humanities
   Project' (London, Heinemann), p. 6.
5 Nordenbo, S.E. (1978), Pluralism, Relativism and the Neutral Teacher, 'Proceedings of the Philosophy of Education
   Society', vol. 12, p. 131.
6 See Testing Times for the Chinese, in 'Times Higher Educational Supplement', 14 December 1979, no. 373, p. 5.
7 Phillips, D.Z. (1974), Another Outbreak of Misology, 'Education for Teaching', no. 95 (Autumn).

Part three
AUTONOMY AND LEARNING

8 EDUCATION AND THE ETHICS OF BELIEF

I

Should we be teaching an 'ethics of belief' in our educational institutions?   Presupposed by our answering this question is a clear understanding of what such an ethics could be.   For if an 'ethics of belief' were a logical impossibility, then the practical question of whether we should be teaching it would obviously be pointless.   We might in that case as well ask whether we should be teaching children to square the circle. If, on the other hand, sense could be given to the phrase, and still more if an excellent achievement were thus marked out as possible, then we should be more likely to hit the mark in realising that possibility if we were clearer what it was.   1 shall, therefore, in the greater part of this paper be concerned with investigating the prior question of possibility, only at the end drawing some practical conclusions on whether we should or should not be teaching anything that might be called an ethics of belief.

II

In contemplating the possibility of an ethics of belief, two major difficulties immediately loom up which seem to make such a notion both misguided and misconceived.   The first of these difficulties concerns the broad distinction which we are ordinarily inclined to make between thought and action, or, roughly speaking, between what goes on in our minds and what we do in the world.   For in the terms of this broad and rather crude distinction we ordinarily think of action as being the proper sphere for an ethics.   What is appropriate to belief is not ethics but logic.   Our thoughts are something which we ordinarily regard as a private matter, and our thinking and what we think are regarded as properly to be left free. Surely at least our minds are our own?

   Action, however, is an overt bringing about of changes in the world, or sometimes a failure to prevent such changes. And these changes frequently have effects on others, touching their interests in many ways.   That is why an ethics, perhaps in some areas backed by legal sanctions, is appropriate.   But what goes on in our heads does not itself have any such effects, and if it leads to actions, then it is these actions which

will be of ethical interest.   Thus, for example, a teacher may
think what he likes on political questions, but when he moves
into action by teaching his opinions to his classes, then others
acquire a legitimate interest in what he is doing.   In Muriel
Spark's 'The Prime of Miss Jean Brodie', that lady would have
been allowed to think what she liked about fascism, but when
she started to persuade her pupils to enter the Spanish Civil
War, her actions gave cause for legitimate alarm.

This broad distinction between thought and action is behind
much of our thinking about censorship.   For in considering
whether to censor some book, film, or theatre production, the
question that is asked, as a legitimate question to ask, is
whether such publication will do any harm.   But 'harm' is
then construed in terms of certain effects on people's actions,
for example in causing them to commit rape, theft or other
acts of violence against persons or property.   The question
is whether the public viewing of, say, Kubrick's 'Clockwork
Orange' will have harmful effects such as these.   But effects
solely on people's thoughts are ignored.   Whether people exposed to such works will be more prone to engage in sadistic
fantasies, lustful imaginings, or dreams of power is beyond
the scope of legitimate ethical concern, provided always that
their mental goings-on do not spill over into action.   You may
think what you like.

If we break down that distinction as the notion of an 'ethics
of belief' would seem to invite us to do, then surely it is only
a short step to various well-known and well-charted social
evils.   It would be only a short step backward to all the
evils of religious heresy-hunting, or only a short step forward
to '1984'.   In Orwell's future people had to learn the 'virtue'
of 'crimestop', which embraced both the ability and the disposition to stop on the threshold of what were sensed to be
particularly dangerous thoughts.   For those who were less
than wholly virtuous in this respect there were the 'thought
police', unrestrained either by principle or by patience from
first waiting to see if such dangerous thoughts would lead to
action.   Ethics, and more particularly moral obligations, may
be relevant to what we *say* that we believe, as perhaps with
lawyers, and it may be relevant to acting *as if* we believed,
as with statesmen in crises, but to be concerned with what is
actually believed, *qua* belief, is a misguided intrusion into
individual privacy.   That is the first major difficulty.

A second difficulty would seem to make such a concern not
merely misguided but even misconceived.   For to believe that
'p' is to believe that 'p is true'.   To believe that rote learning is uneducational, or that the earth is slightly pear-shaped,
or that the square of seven is forty-nine, is to believe these
propositions to be true.   The question of whether or not to
believe them is therefore the same as the question whether or

not to regard them as true.   But that is a question which is
properly to be settled only by logically relevant appraisals of
those propositions.   The truth and appropriateness of the
reasons that might back them up, and the validity of any in-
ferences made in backing them up, are what we should
properly be concerned with, not the supposed ethics of
believing that 'p' or that 'not-p'.

The same difficulty can be viewed in another way.   It is a
widely accepted maxim that 'ought implies can'.   In the terms
of our present interest this would mean that an ethics of
belief implies (presupposes) that we can, as an act of will,
believe or not believe that p.   But believing is no such act
of will.   There is no imperative 'believe that p!' such that
we could know how to obey it.   Nor do we believe on purpose, or deliberately, or intentionally, or for the sake of anything.   So how could any ethical 'ought' be appropriate to
the believing of 'p', or of 'not-p'?   The notion of an ethics
of belief is not just misguided, through its intrusion into the
privacy of our minds, but it is misconceived because it would
ask of us what in any case we could not do. (1)

III

There are, however, some arguments that might be put on the
other side, though with what success it remains to be seen.
For, on second thoughts, we do sometimes speak of belief in
a way which seems to connect it with the will.   We speak of
'refusing' to believe, of finding something 'easy' or 'difficult'
to believe, and of feeling 'inclined' or 'disinclined' to believe.
But locutions such as these could be interpreted as express-
ing the different degrees of readiness and confidence with
which we do or do not assent to a proposition.   Such differences of degree would be correlative to the weight or force of
evidence, not expressive of our degree of determination to
believe.

Thus to be 'unable' to believe, or to find 'difficulty' in
believing, is not to suffer from some obscure defect of will,
or to be in need of urging to try harder.   It is a more cognitive matter of finding the evidence unacceptable, or unsatis-
factory, in its bearings on the proposition in question.   If I
find it hard to believe, as I do, that differences in intelligence
are wholly attributable to differences in environmental advantage, then it is no weakness of will which makes it hard.   It
is the abundance of apparently contrary evidence.

Nevertheless, assent is surely a mental act, even a species
of decision.   At the end of a process of reflection or inquiry
we may wish to 'make up our minds'.   Having looked at the
evidence on, say, the question of streaming (or tracking)

children by ability in schools, it remains to decide where that
evidence points.   Do I assent to the proposition that, all
things considered, streaming is rightly discredited, or do I
not so assent?   But if something of the nature of a decision
attaches to such assent, it is nevertheless still logical and
not ethical appraisals which are relevant to the making of that
decision.   Of course, ethical considerations may be amongst
the many other considerations bearing on the belief, but those
ethical considerations will still bear logically on that belief.
The kind of reflective decision which we call 'assent' is a
decision *that* something is the case, based on a review of
logically relevant considerations of various sorts (including
sometimes the ethical sort, of course).

A bolder, if cruder, attempt to represent belief as a species
of action, and so within the normal sphere of ethics, would
rest on behaviouristic presuppositions about the nature of
mind.   Thus 'believing that p' might be construed in terms
of a behavioural disposition to do a certain range of things.
To believe that the cat wants to come in might be construed
as being disposed to go and unlock the back door, or to go
to the front door and call 'puss, puss', or to say 'yes' in
response to any question as to whether the cat wants to come
in, etc.   Such behavioural doings could clearly be the subject of ethical concern, especially if one thought that animals
had rights, or if, more weakly, one thought that there was
an imperfect duty to be kind to animals.   And, in favour of
a behaviouristic account of belief, we can certainly say that it
is normally from what people say and do (i.e. from their
behaviour) that we know what they believe.   How else might
I know that my wife thinks the cat wants to come in?

Still, the force of the argument could be read as going in
the other direction.   That is to say, if behaviourism has as
one of its logical consequences that an ethics of belief would
be possible, then, because such an ethics is impossible, pointing out that consequence would be yet another nail in the
behaviourist coffin.   But that reversal of the argument takes
for granted the validity of our earlier arguments to show an
ethics of belief to be misguided and misconceived.   It would
therefore be less tendentious if separate reasons were given
for rejecting behaviourist analyses of belief.   Such reasons
are not hard to find, though only some of them will be stated
here, and with a brevity appropriate to their familiarity and
to their minor place in this paper. (2)

First there is the difficulty, similar to that of phenomenalist
accounts of perception, of satisfactorily specifying the class of
behaviours constitutive of a given belief.   For one wants to
say that it is precisely the belief, as something separate from
the behaviours, which gives the class its unity.   There is an

openness to the class of behaviours expressive of such a
belief as that the cat wants to come in.   Any list will inevitably have to be terminated with a vague 'etc.' for which no
rule can be given that would enable us to go on.   In any
case, we can for our own part know what we believe without
first seeing how we are disposed to behave.   I can know
that I believe that whales can communicate for distances up to
seven hundred miles without investigating anything that I am
disposed to do.   In fact, like many other beliefs of mine
picked up from television, this one is for practical purposes
idle.

Not only can we not classify the behaviours supposedly
equivalent to a belief, but we cannot identify any particular
piece of behaviour as behaviour of a given sort apart from
knowing the person's beliefs.   Is this man who is running
along the road an escaping thief, or is he hastening to catch
the train?   Perhaps he is just taking some vigorous exercise,
or hurrying to get home before the storm breaks?   The
nature of what he is doing depends on, rather than is par-
tially equivalent to, what he believes.   Furthermore, beliefs
have to be able to explain our passivity as well as our activity, our involuntary reactions as well as our purposeful endeavouring.   Thus, blushes, trembling and knee-knockings
are explained by our beliefs, as well as our voluntary behaviour.   And finally, there is the familiar point that believing
can be distinguished from pretending to believe, though in
form they may be behaviourally identical.

All roads to an ethics of belief therefore seem to be blocked.
In the light of our ordinary distinction between thought and
action, and the maxim that 'ought implies can', such a notion
seems both misguided and misconceived.   Apparent connections with the will made through references to ease or difficulty, and assent, do not damage the point that only logical
appraisals are appropriate to any reflective decision as to
what to believe.   And finally, behaviourist reductions aimed
at reducing beliefs to behavioural dispositions are open to the
many objections to behaviourism itself.   It therefore looks as
if the question of whether we should be teaching an ethics of
belief just does not arise.

IV

In 'Novum Organon', Francis Bacon makes the following remark:
'The human understanding is no dry light, but receives an infusion from the will and affections;   whence proceed sciences
which may be called "sciences as one would".' (3)   The point
of this remark about the understanding 'receiving an infusion',
with various effects, is that what we believe can be determined

by very different factors.   So far in this paper the sorts of
reasons which have been assumed to be operative are logically
relevant reasons.   It has been assumed that appropriate evidence will be given due weight in determining what to believe,
or in determining where we shall give our assent.   Thus if
we were considering whether to follow Ivan Illich in believing
that society should be de-schooled, then the task would be to
assess the truth and validity of his arguments: that schools
are 'manipulative' institutions, that they produce gross inequalities of opportunity, that the freedom to purchase chosen
educational resources would avoid these evils, etc.

But of course, 'the human understanding is no dry light',
and in the determination of what we shall believe many factors
besides those which are logically relevant may be operative.
Our beliefs may simply represent a rather passive acquies-
cence in the face of social pressures.   Parents, teachers,
advertisements, or the media may have left their deposits in
our minds, or even more forcefully have drummed or dinned
beliefs into us, and all without any assessment of truth or
validity on our part.   The 'other-directed' man may well be
quite as 'other-directed' in what he thinks as in what he does.

Again, our beliefs may be determined, not by other people,
but by our own wishes, desires and emotions, and again without any reference to criteria for the appraisal of such beliefs.
My desire not to admit that I have made a bad buy in pur-
chasing this second-hand car may induce me to believe that it
really has all sorts of non-existent virtues.   My mood of nostalgia about army life may engender quite untrue beliefs about
the excellence of barrack room life and all the good times that
went with it.   Rose-tinted spectacles are, after all, placed on
our own noses, not forcibly thrust there by others.

But if what we believe can be determined by such a wide
diversity of factors, then perhaps here is a more promising
possibility for an ethics of belief.   For we can exercise control over those factors, allowing or disallowing, giving or refusing them influence in the making up of our minds.   Considerations which have logical relevance to certain beliefs can
thus be given normative force in the psychology of the individual.   Evidence and argument can thus be given preponder-
ant weight in determining our assent and the degrees of confidence with which we assent.   Spinoza amongst traditional
philosophers has perhaps given most attention to this possibility, and he entitled his chief work on it 'Ethics'.

An ethics of belief, then, could capitalise on the fact that
we *can* exercise control over the factors determining what we
believe.   And it would then go beyond this possibility in indicating how we actually ought to control these factors.

Thus an ethics of belief would have nothing directly to say
about the content of what we ought to believe, for as was
argued earlier, only logical appraisals are appropriate there.
Whether to believe that p is the same as the question whether
p is true, and that question in turn is properly to be determined by the weight of evidence or argument.   But giving
weight to evidence or argument, and doing so perhaps in the
face of social pressures, or the pull of one's wishes, desires
and emotions, can properly be an object of normative control.

This was indeed broadly the view of W.K. Clifford, who
appears to have been the originator of the phrase, though not
the concept, 'ethics of belief'.   Clifford wrote:

The question of right or wrong has to do with the origin of
his belief, not the matter of it;   not what it was, but how
he got it;   not whether it turned out to be true or false,
but whether he had a right to believe on such evidence as
was before him. (4)

There can, therefore, be normative requirements for the
proper *formation* of beliefs, just as there can be normative requirements of an admittedly paradigmatic ethical kind for the
control of our actions.   Because the mental processes of
belief-formation are often largely, and sometimes wholly,
covert, there may be a disinclination to refer to those processes as constituting 'action', but they are certainly activities and they may terminate in acts.   While all of this is no
warrant at all for interfering with other people's belief-formation, it does at least show a possible sphere for an autono-
mously applied ethics.   It might be a sphere of duties to oneself, for example.

The norms of such a possible ethics would have two sources.
One of these would be the logic relevant to the kinds of belief
being formed: mathematical, empirical, moral, technically
practical, etc.   Thus true mathematical beliefs must be
deducible from certain axioms, true empirical beliefs must
accord with certain observation statements, true moral beliefs
must (perhaps) give due weight to considerations picked out
by certain principles, while technically practical beliefs must
accord with a complexity of criteria for teleological efficacy.
Since the present purpose is only one of illustration, commitment to any particular epistemological position on the logic of
different forms of thought is not vital.

A second source for an ethics of belief would be the psychology of the individual.   It would refer to the typical human
proclivities for going wrong in various ways in forming beliefs.
Differences in intelligence relevant to ease or difficulty in
understanding would not be relevant to such an ethics

directly, but they would be indirectly relevant to the capacities assumed to be present as a presupposition of applicability. 'Ought implies can' here too.   The sorts of proclivities which would be relevant would be those mentioned earlier as alternative formative influences in our beliefs: proclivities towards being influenced by the irrelevant pressure of others, or the pull of our own wishes, desires and emotions.

V

Clearly, then, there is scope for normative requirements bearing on the activities by which we do, or can, form our beliefs.   But why call such requirements 'ethical'?   Why not simply regard them as technical rules for the forming of true beliefs, if true beliefs are what we want?   Clearly there are *some* cases where carefulness or carelessness in forming our beliefs is of quite ordinary ethical concern, because of the things which we do in the light of those beliefs.   The major ethical concern is with action, but action cannot be divorced from belief, as indeed our own arguments against behaviourism were explicitly designed to show.

Take ordinary moral action, for example.   It is not moral action if we do the morally right thing by accident, or through its coincidence with really operative self-interested reasons. Moral action is done for moral reasons, and those moral reasons embrace beliefs.   If there are moral obligations at all, then presumably there are derivative moral obligations to try to form corresponding true moral beliefs, since only through such beliefs can our moral obligations be discharged in a moral way.   It is no excuse to say that I did not know cruelty to be wrong, or that it had not crossed my mind that driving while drunk might have a significance beyond that of attracting the tiresome attention of the police.   I ought to have known.   It ought to have crossed my mind.   My conscience ought to be submitted to some degree of scrutiny. Thus the discerning of moral obligations ought to be one area of belief-formation of genuinely ethical concern.

So far, however, it is only the forming of moral beliefs which has been argued to be of properly ethical, and not just of technical concern.   But in fact forming *any* belief could be of ethical concern.   This could be so in situations where a person speaks with trusted authority, as do teachers on at least some occasions in our educational institutions.   Such a teacher is no doubt under the same obligation as anybody else to speak the truth, or rather not to speak untruth since silence is also a possibility.   But as a trusted authority, the more trusted the greater the immaturity of the learners, he has a special obligation to make as sure as he reasonably can

that what he says *is* the truth.   But the content of what he
says might have nothing to do with others at all.   In effect,
his obligation is to teach as true only what he sincerely
believes, and to give it his carefully considered judgement
before teaching it.

The case of the trusted authority can be widened.   Other
occasions of public statement-making can be included which
call for a prior scrutiny of what one thinks that is rather
more rigorous than is required by the quite general obligation
not to speak untruths.   Statements having legal significance
come into this category, such as evidence given in a court.
Public accusations prejudicial to the credit or reputation of
others are further examples.   In such ways as these, then,
the forming or holding of *any* belief could become the subject
of ethical scrutiny, though in practice some beliefs are unlikely to gain this sort of attention.   Yet even if these
arguments are valid, what we then have in practice is an
ethical concern only with some beliefs, and therefore a concern only with some of the ethics of belief which our previous
arguments showed to be possible.   Could a wider concern
with our beliefs be properly regarded as ethical?

If our ordinary ethics of action is built round the dignity
and intrinsic worth of persons, then its various principles
can be seen as so many specifications of what it is to have
respect for persons.   Could there not be a comparable ethics
of belief built round the dignity and intrinsic worth of truth,
with its normative requirements so many specifications of what
it is to have respect for truth?   'Respect for truth' need not
imply valuing any and every particular true proposition, no
matter how trivial or irrelevant to any of our interests it may
be.   But it would imply that if any particular belief were,
for one reason or another, of significance to us, then it
would be a matter of intrinsic concern that it should be a true
belief.   A roughly comparable selectivity applies in the case
of persons.

Two questions that arise here are: 'Why respect truth as
something of intrinsic worth?' and 'Why should such respect,
if granted, be regarded as ethical?'   I shall try to answer
only the second question since the first raises issues dispro-
portionately large for the purposes of this paper.   Briefly
then, an ethics of belief would be built round the intrinsic
worth of truth as a human value.   It would be regarded as
an ethics for the further reasons that the language of the
normative requirements involved is the same as the language
of ordinary ethics, and that the effects of observing those
normative requirements are effects on character.

Of course, it would be ridiculously severe to call a man

immoral simply because of a proneness to wishful thinking, or
simply because he was so easily open to persuasion by others.
But it would be equally ridiculous to call a man immoral for
some deficiencies in the ordinary ethics of action, for example
for being ungenerous or unforgiving.   Again, to establish an
ethics of belief need no more warrant Orwellian or heresy-
hunting interferences with others than ordinary social morality
warrants such interferences.   Privacy can still be a value,
including the privacy of one's thoughts.   We do not necessarily think legal interference is warranted even for such
breaches of ordinary social morality as telling lies, breaking
promises, or unkindness, unless these occur in certain special
contexts.

But illustrations are needed of the brief argument to justify
calling normative requirements for belief 'ethical'.   It was
suggested that the language was the same as for the ethics of
action, and that the effects were equally effects on character.
Thus, amongst the *virtues* correlative to an ethics of belief
would be doing justice to a view, showing patience with the
difficulties which stand in the way of reaching a conclusion,
having the humility to recognise a need to learn, restraining
one's natural passion for certainty, and controlling one's
natural impulsiveness to believe what is immediately congenial
to believe.   There would also be open-mindedness, in the
sense of being accessible to criticism and being open to influence by counter-evidence and counter-argument.   Further
virtues would be integrity in the face of social pressures, and
courage in facing the perhaps depressing implications of the
truth of a belief.

The range of corresponding vices is equally great.   It includes credulity, gullibility, superstition, wishful thinking,
self-deception and many forms of bias and prejudice.   It is
in terms of such virtues and vices as these that we may praise
or blame someone for thinking as he does.   The language of
rights and obligations also has a place.   Thus a person's
'right to believe' something may be highly questionable, while
A.J. Ayer includes amongst the conditions for knowledge that
we have 'the right to be sure'.   We may sensibly say that we
are normatively 'obliged' to believe that 'p', or (normatively
again) obliged to accept what is said by some authority judged
to be good.

Of course, some areas of truth are not just of private concern but are of public and indeed institutionalised importance.
This at least ought to be the case with the press, with com-
mittees of inquiry and with courts.   In cases such as these,
the boundary between an ethics of belief and a particular
application of interpersonal or social morality is hard to draw.
Such institutions typically also embody devices and procedures

representative of a suspicion that individual virtue may often
be imperfect, so that more certain public safeguards of truth
have to be found.   Again, these public institutionalised forms
of respect for truth may well be psychologically necessary as
a model for the individual to internalise.

VI

What is the educational importance of the ethics of belief?
The first thing that might be said in answer to that question
is that some practices in our schools make no sense except on
the assumption that such an ethics is of proper concern.   I
refer to praising and blaming for the quality of the academic
work that is done.   When, for example, children are praised
for a piece of reasoning, or blamed for some sloppiness in
failing to exercise proper care in a calculation or experiment,
then it is virtues and vices which are being presupposed.
If the praising and blaming are just, then it is merits or deficiencies of acquired character which are being judged.

The question has also been answered by the various curriculum development projects in Britain and the USA which make
critical discussion the central point of a learning activity.
Of course this is nothing new at the level of higher education,
where the ethics of belief finds its paradigmatic institutionalised forms.   But it is still something of a novelty at the
school level, where a tradition of authoritarian teaching has
been until quite recently all but universal, and still flourishes
in places.

Much needless controversy over the possibility and desirability of the 'neutral teacher' could have been avoided if the
notion of an ethics of belief had first been made an object of
more explicit awareness.   This controversy has arisen in
England over Lawrence Stenhouse's Humanities Curriculum Project, in which discussion is a central activity and in which the
'teacher' has the role of 'neutral chairman'.   But then what
is he teaching, it has been asked.   And if there is discussion, how can he be neutral on truth and rationality?   A
careful reading of Stenhouse's writing, however, soon shows
that the teacher is not to be neutral on the ethics of belief.
In fact, that is exactly what he is teaching, especially a critical attitude to evidence.   His 'neutrality' is the procedural
tactic, familiar to all seminar leaders, of facilitating thorough
discussion of a controversial topic by not oneself expressly
favouring one side of the argument, whatever one substantively thinks.   The task is to gain a hearing for views, while
ensuring that those views are both presented and discussed
with due regard to the intrinsic values of a critical, truth-
seeking attitude.   On these values no neutrality is intended. (5)

So, with more or less flickering awareness, and sporadical-
ly, the ethics of belief is being taught in our schools as something of importance.   And, quite apart from its attracting
attention in controversial areas of the curriculum, it can be
seen to be an important ingredient in such much less intrinsically controversial areas as mathematics and science.   For
many of the newer approaches to teaching in these areas are
concerned not just to transmit information, or even an established body of knowledge, but to involve the learner in thinking, albeit embryonically, like a mathematician or a scientist,
with due regard to various normative requirements.   At least
two important values are involved here, quite apart from any
social or technological utilities.   These values are the particular curricular form of thought itself, for example mathematics,
and also personal autonomy, or directing one's mind and action
by reference to one's own independent judgement.   The ethics
of belief is the offspring of neither alone, but of the union of
the two.

It might be said that really all I have been discussing is the
intellectual virtues, which, far from being new, were quite
familiar even to Aristotle.   And in a way it would be quite
correct to say this.   But in preferring to call such virtues
the virtues of an *ethics* of belief I have had it in mind to
emphasise an aspect of this old idea that is too often neglected
in schooling.   This is that a development of character, not
just a topping up with accurate information, is required.   We
may have a picture of the mind as so permeable by reason that
only perfect clarity in presentation is required of the teacher,
coupled no doubt with an ability to keep order.   So long as
the content and logic of a form of thought are accurately displayed, whether in oral teaching or written comments, then
the reception of these furnishings into the cabinet of the mind
may be assumed.   To change the metaphor a little, it is
thought that if only we are clear and accurate as teachers in
our presentation, then the learner will be able to gaze upon
and thus to know what we display without either obscurity or
obstruction.

But what if the understanding is 'no dry light'?   What if it
'receives an infusion from the will and affections'?   Then in
that case the entry of reason into the mind will only be effected by something of a struggle in which it has to contend with
many adversaries, as Spinoza and Bacon knew so well.   Consider some of the 'problems' encountered by Oliver and Bane
in attempting to discuss controversial issues in US schools:

Although students sometimes become very excited about the
issues raised by the cases, they seldom seem to take the
issues seriously in a personal sense.   They enjoy the
combat of discussion and the opportunity to express their

> opinions, but they are not generally sensitive to the argu-
> ments of other people ... the discussion becomes a repetition
> of opinions rather than an attempt at clarification ... a game
> in which the object is either to second-guess the teacher
> and arrive at the right answer or to overwhelm the other
> participants psychologically. (6)

Clearly the 'problem' here is more than one of demisting the
mental windscreen.

The 'intellectual virtues' are no mere accuracies of vision,
but are aspects of character developed in contending with
Baconian idols.   Greek ideas of the theoretical 'part of the
soul' as being serenely contemplative of divinely unchanging
realities have left their legacy of unfortunate metaphor to mislead the teacher in trying to understand his task.   No doubt
there are important differences between theoretical and practical reason, but both have to become realities in our minds
against inclinations, against the pull of certain wishes and
desires, and in the face of certain pressures from other
people.   Both Aristotle's so-called 'intellectual' and his
'moral' virtues are developments of character, and both involve
habituation as well as teaching.   I would say that both involve the teaching of an ethics, though in the one case an
ethics of belief.

REFERENCES

1 This last point was suggested to me by reading R. Edgley's
   'Reason in Theory and Practice' (1969, London, Hutchinson).
2 See A. Phillips Griffiths, On Belief, in 'Proceedings of the
   Aristotelian Society', 1962-3.
3 F. Bacon, 'Novum Organon', Book One, XLIX.
4 W.K. Clifford (1879), 'Lectures and Essays', vol. 2
   (London, Macmillan), p. 178.
5 See the symposium by C. Bailey and J. Elliott, Teaching by
   Discussion and the Neutral Teacher, in 'Proceedings of the
   Philosophy of Education Society of Great Britain', vol. 7,
   no. 1, January 1973, pp. 26-64.
6 D.W. Oliver and M.J. Bane, Moral education: is reasoning
   enough?, in 'Moral Education', eds C.M. Beck, B.S. Crit-
   tenden, and B.V. Sullivan, University of Toronto Press,
   p. 260.

9 AUTONOMY AND INTELLECTUAL EDUCATION

I

In the course of reflecting on the nature of autonomy over a
number of years, I have changed my mind about it in some
respects but not in others.   When I wrote my 'Philosophy of
Primary Education' I was at my most optimistic, hoping that at
least the broad outlines of the curriculum could somehow be
derived from autonomy as the central principle of education. (1)   I no longer think that.   It now seems to me
obvious that at least morality requires a separate root, since
it is perfectly possible, conceptually, for a person to be
highly autonomous yet amoral.   The rational egoist is a case
in point.   Further assumptions have also to be made before
other directions can be determined in which autonomy might
be developed.

In my article Autonomy and Education I gave a skeletal
account of autonomy as being achieved by a person 'to the
degree that what he thinks and does cannot be explained
without reference to his own activity of mind'. (2)   Elaborating on this in a subsequent article, I suggested three criteria
for regarding a person as autonomous: (1) that he forms his
own judgements on what to think and do; (2) that he is disposed critically to reflect on his own first-order judgements;
and (3) that he is disposed to integrate his actual belief and
conduct round these first-order and reflective judgements. (3)
As some critics have been quick to point out, this account
raises difficulties in knowing when a person is in fact autonomous, while making clear the supposed value of autonomy is a
further difficulty. (4)   But it is a somewhat different aspect
that I would like to consider on this occasion.   This aspect
can be introduced by a brief consideration of autonomy in relation to child-centred educational theory.

Probably the central idea in child-centred theorising is that
of growth.   In Froebel, for example, one finds human nature
regarded as an inner latency which will unfold and develop
given the right sort of environment.   A close analogy is seen
between the teacher and the gardener, and Froebel stresses
the crucial importance of spotting often indistinct budding
points which mark the incipient emergence of a new and educationally valuable interest.   Although there are some

passages discordant with this general picture of respect for pupil self-activity, as when Froebel says of a child marred by his environment that in that circumstance 'directly categorical, mandatory education in its full severity is demanded', (5) in general, the original Froebelian picture is one of following immanent 'laws of growth'.

Much in this picture is appropriate, especially with the youngest children. Physical maturation is like this and, even though it must be distinguished in many ways from mental development, at least it implies the sequential emergence of necessary conditions for mental development. The 'budding point' notion marks the importance of capitalising on existing or newly sparked interests. The stress on self-activity intimates an anti-authoritarianism which appears to sit well with regarding autonomy as important.

There are, however, also some difficulties in this model of education. Without rehearsing them all, the one to which I would most draw attention is the apparent underestimation of social influences and what we inherit from traditions. The most autonomous of men owes far more to what he socially inherits than to what he makes of himself, and the ideal of autonomy is itself a product of one particular social tradition. In our general knowledge too, far more of what we learn is mediated by language and traditions of inquiry than ever could be acquired by independent discovery. As Quinton expresses it in a graphic image, society is like a grocer, not only in supplying us with our principal stores but also in supplying us with the scales on which to weigh them. (6) There is also the point that if the development of autonomy is to come to its proper fruition, it needs to be complemented by appropriate political and economic institutions. On this, the European child-centred tradition is largely silent, though Dewey had a great deal to say about it.

I remarked earlier that the younger the children, the more appropriate is the child-centred model. Much of the detailed content of early learning fits the picture quite well, especially when learning is close to the perception of what is immediately to hand. But properly intellectual development requires what R.S. Peters calls 'initiation' into socially transmitted traditions of inquiry. In some versions, child-centred theory not only fails to provide an adequate account of such an intellectual education but is also actually hostile to it. This was not so with Dewey, though he rather restricted intellectual activity to practical and widely shared concerns. But A.S. Neill, for example, was so preoccupied with emotional development as to give no important place to intellectual development at all. 'If the emotions are free,' he wrote, 'the intellect will look after itself.' (7) Froebel also appears to have been somewhat

ambivalent towards intellectual activity.   His own thought
runs off into mysticism, strange word plays, and the revelation of an intuitively held vision.   But I want to argue that,
whatever may be the place of intellectual education in child-
centred theories, a continuous concern for it across the whole
span of education, from primary school to university, is one
of the chief educational ways of pursuing autonomy as an ideal.

II

I take it that with intellectual as with any other sort of development, the nature of the earlier stages can best be appreciated by looking at the final accomplishment.   In the present
case, it will perhaps be sufficient by way of indicating the
scope of intellectual education if I say that it consists of such
studies as you find most fully developed in a university.
These will include the whole range of the pure and applied
sciences, histories of this and that, languages and their associated literatures, mathematics, law, geography, philosophy and
so on.

Intellectual education implies first of all making acquaintance
with a range of cognitive content: certain concepts, facts,
principles, theories, problems, interpretations and patterns of
explanation and justification.   But it is not just a matter of
loading up with cognitive freight.   It implies also an endeavour towards precision, articulateness, order and an interrela-
tion between the parts.   It especially implies an activity of
critical discernment as content is sifted, evaluated and in
general critically assessed.   Truth, consistency and adequacy
are constantly questioned and there is a corresponding alertness to falsehood, invalidity and inadequacy.   An uncritical
intellectual is a contradiction.   It is this activity of critical
thinking which makes intellectual education also a development
of autonomy.

A question that naturally arises here is whether this critical
thinking which is such an essential part of intellectual activity
is a general skill, transferable from one field of intellectual
endeavour to another.   Some of those who have written on
this question most recently have denied the very possibility
of such generality.   Both P.H. Hirst (8) and J. McPeck, (9)
for example, have claimed that the appropriate criteria of
judgement, as well as the detailed knowledge content, will be
specific to a particular field.   While a person might learn to
be critical in several fields, it would therefore be something
separate and distinguishable which he would have to learn in
each case.   Furthermore, specialised intellectual activity is
now so much the order of the day that the term 'an intellectual' is rapidly losing the currency it once had.   The strain

shows in attempts to formulate a modern conception of liberal education.

In some ways philosophy might itself lay claim to the role of giving a general intellectual training in critical thinking, but it does not get very far on the basis of formal logic alone. To get to grips with actual problems, philosophy presupposes some awareness of the concrete field in which the problem arises, whether it is science, mathematics, history, education, law, or whatever. The illusion of being a purely general critical skill is fostered by a reliance on commonsense examples, such as are abundantly available in the consideration of morals and everyday perception and memory.

While it may well be true that nothing general could ever be sufficient for tackling intellectual problems, that is not to say that nothing general is necessary, or even possible. At least a set of expectations and attitudes might be developed in one field of intellectual activity which were appropriately transferable to other fields. For example, there might be a general alertness to the proper bases of claims and to different kinds of appropriate evidence. Distinctions such as those between authority and evidence, or fact and value, might have general application. Formal logic could be the source of at least some general skills. What I am suggesting is that there is an important fallacy in arguments on this topic. It lies in moving from the correct observation that general features could never be sufficient, to the conclusion that therefore they can never have any place at all.

If this account of intellectual activity is correct so far, then intellectual education cannot simply be a matter of getting within earshot of the teacher, or commanding an unobstructed view of the blackboard. There are, for example, skills to be acquired which can only be acquired by practice and critical commentary upon that.

One of the highroads to intellectual education lies in dealing with controversial issues, whether current or historical. By a 'controversial issue' I do not mean something on which one man's opinion is as good as another's or which, as a simple matter of social fact, is disputed. I mean something on which contrary views can be held without being contrary to reason. Typically each view then has something to be said for it, but that something falls short of a fully satisfactory account, especially in not decisively dealing with alternative views. (10)

The existence of controversy is commonly regarded by practical men as disappointing, because they want clear and unambiguous answers in order to release their practical energies to

best effect.   Yet argument and discussion are the life-blood
of intellectual activity, and the outbreak of controversy may
itself mark a major step forward towards a more adequate conception, a better understanding, even truth itself.   Tackling
controversial issues in education, in any subject or across
subject boundaries, would avoid that misrepresentation of our
knowledge as being monolithic and authoritative, something
upon which one only has to consult the relevant book or
expert for certainty to be revealed.

It is quite possible to acquire knowledge of a sort without
developing intellectually, or acquiring anything much in the
way of critical alertness.   Everything may be taken on authority.   It may even be that stock criticisms and standard
objections are learned, as in the cleverest kinds of indoctrination.   Someone may be trained merely with a view to his
becoming an efficient operative after some standard pattern.
Training such as this may even have a useful place in the
overall scheme of things, but it is not intellectual education.
The liberalising element of critical alertness is absent, nor is
there any growth in intellectual autonomy.   It is especially
through the activities of critical sifting and discernment that
we make knowledge in a strong sense 'our own', integrating it
into our general understanding and conduct.

Before proceeding further I will draw together my argument
so far.   I began by giving a skeletal account of autonomy in
terms of the three features of making independent judgements,
a disposition critically to reflect on these judgements and a
disposition to integrate belief and conduct round these independent and reflective judgements.   I saw some analogies
between this and the growth concept of child-centred theory
but also some points of difference.   These were sharpened by
considering the nature of intellectual development as it proceeds through schooling and on to college or university.
Intellectual education has critical thinking as its life-blood and
it is this that justifies regarding it as one of the chief educational ways of pursuing autonomy as an ideal.

III

Child-centred theories typically refer to the many-sidedness of
child development: the physical, social, spiritual, emotional
and moral as well as the intellectual.   With this many-sidedness in mind, a natural reaction to what I have said so far
about intellectual education might be to criticise it as being
altogether too exclusively one-sided.   This is a criticism
which I would like to consider at some length.

Because intellectual activity is closely concerned with truth,

or with the objectivity and correctness of judgements, it has
sometimes been supposed to be somewhat removed from any
exercise of the imagination.   In his novel 'Hard Times',
Dickens contrasted literalness and closeness to fact with
giving freer play to the imagination or fancy.   Gradgrind
remonstrates with Cecilia Jupe as follows, in a chapter entitled
'murdering the innocents':

> you are to be in all things regulated and governed by fact.
> We hope, before long, a *board* of fact, composed of *commis-
> sioners* of fact, who will force the people to be a *people* of
> fact, and nothing but fact.   You must discard the word
> Fancy altogether.   You have nothing to do with it.   You
> are not to have, in any object or ornament, what would be
> a contradiction of fact. (11)

What this reign of fact would be like is later indicated when
Gradgrind advises his 20-year-old daughter on how she should
respond to 50-year-old Bounderby's proposal of marriage.
He recommends that they consult the statistical tables for mar-
riages between partners of such unequal ages.

Yet to make such a stark contrast is a misconception.   If
we take science as a paradigm of intellectual activity, then all
of its most striking achievements represent great feats of the
imagination.   If, for example, we took the theories of Darwin,
Freud, Copernicus, Galileo, Harvey or Einstein as instances,
then in each case prodigious use of the imagination was necessary.   The contrary error arises from failing to distinguish
the process of inquiry from the eventually established results.
Inquiry is always dependent on imagination for possible explanations, conjectures, interpretations or new perspectives.
Even to envisage a new line of criticism within existing knowledge involves an exercise of imagination.   As John Passmore
says, critical thinking requires imagination if real possibilities
are to be seen, and imagination needs critical thinking if it is
not just to be fanciful. (12)

There are in the Andes of South America desert areas in
which a pattern of long straight lines can be seen.   An explanation that has been offered of these lines is that they are
the remains of landing strips used by ancient space travellers.
But that is an explanation undisciplined by critical thinking.
It is merely fanciful.   The true explanation appears to be
that the lines represent a kind of calendar by which a former
culture knew the cycle of the seasons.   This explanation can
be and has been critically tested by correlation with astronom-
ical observations.   True or not, in some sense it represents
a greater feat of imagination to conceive and test this possibility than the easy and merely fanciful spaceship story.

If intellectual activity is contrasted with imagination to show
it as an exclusively one-sided emphasis in education, then a
great injustice is done to the nature of intellectual activity.
While it is true that some flights of imagination are merely
fanciful from the point of view of intellectual endeavour, in
other respects there is a crucial dependence on imagination.
To regard the sciences, for example, as being the special
habitat of 'convergent thinkers' because of their concern with
finding the true answer, or at any rate the best answer, to
some question, is therefore a mistake.   And it is a mistake
which is probably generated by methods of teaching which
ignore inquiry for results and which ignore controversial
issues for established truths.

IV

Perhaps a more usual accusation of one-sidedness is to the
effect that intellectual education ignores emotional development.
Certainly there is traditionally supposed to be some sort of
incompatibility here.   Intellect may be viewed as a blight on
spontaneous impulse, or as the pale cast of thought which
chills all warmth and humanity.   There have in philosophy
long been arguments over whether reason should be seen as
master or slave of the passions.   Plato imagined the soul as
being like a charioteer pulled by two very different steeds.

It would, I think, be wrong to say that there is no truth
in this familiar opposition.   An intellectual appreciation of
long-term objectives, a firm grasp of general principles, or a
loyalty to the requirements of truth may each conflict with
particular emotions, such as nostalgia or eager impulse.   On
the other side, it has to be said that a human being is fit-
tingly susceptible to certain emotions, such as grief, which
may elude intellectual comprehension in terms of some useful
point.   Again, emotional turmoil may be the necessary medium
through which alone a tightly worked out intellectual scheme
of things, which is nevertheless inadequate in larger human
terms, can be broken up and dislodged from control over a
person's outlook or perspective.

By a suitable choice of examples, it could be argued that
intellectual activity is in certain senses properly dependent
upon emotion.   The experience of certain emotions may be a
necessary condition of seeing some fact, or of attaching proper
weight to certain considerations.   It would be a bold, and
possibly also a rash, person who thought that he could attach
proper weight to all the considerations bearing upon a right
judgement about abortion, say, or unemployment, without
having any direct experience of these things, with all its
emotional impact.

As Spinoza perhaps above all other philosophers knew, intellectual activity is itself sustained by emotion. Nietzsche too, though with different intent, saw the sustaining power of emotion. In a memorable recent passage, R.K. Elliott comes to grips with the problem of finding out what it is that makes for intellectual vitality. He describes the typical phases as an inquirer works on a topic as follows:

> it may begin as an *anxious* sense of being in a region void of life; he experiences the *quickening* of the topic, which alleviates his *anxiety*; the *exhilaration* of following lines of inquiry which open out before him ...; *satisfaction* at the transformation of a feeling of *unease* into an explicit problem, a transformation perhaps long delayed through *dread* of the problem; he experiences the *sense of being enclosed* within a narrow circle of ideas; the *joy* of sudden illumination; *excitement* and *fear* in seizing upon some apparently original idea ...; he feels *insecurity* when the topic seems to be getting out of hand; *dismay* at the proliferation of problems and the confusion this generates ...; *despair* at finding himself outcast from a topic once again void of life. (13) (my italics)

Whether we think of the secondary school pupil doing some history homework, or the university researcher tackling some new problems, these emotional aspects of intellectual activity are immediately recognisable.

As it was found with imagination, so too with emotion, it is altogether too quick and simple to set up a one-sided opposition between intellectual and other sorts of development in a person. There are some incompatibilities in particular cases, but there are also dependencies and sustaining relationships to be discerned.

V

As one final example of the possible one-sidedness of intellectual development, I would like to explore its relationship to morality. Perhaps the first thing that would need to be said here is that it is possible to claim both too much and too little for intellect. It would commonly be thought, with at least apparent justice, that Plato was an example of claiming too much. We are by now much too familiar with the morally ambiguous uses to which science and technology can be put, or the ways in which history can be selectively drawn upon, or even the ways in which mathematical statistics can serve political ideologies, for us readily to suppose that a high-powered intellectual education will necessarily make men good.

Nevertheless, it is to jump too readily to the other extreme
to place exclusive stress on the heart, or the warm effusions
of a sympathy that is undirected by right judgement.   Even
the simplest cases of moral response call for some assessment
of the facts.   Complex institutional implications may call for
very considerable intellectual endeavour if the features of justice are to be critically discerned.   As Hepburn once remarked, if benevolence is wholly confined to intimate personal en-
counters after the style of the Good Samaritan, a quite sense-
less prejudice may result against such things as state-planned
welfare or organised famine relief as being too impersonal or
coldly scientific. (14)

There are, then, once again many connections of a positive
and dependent kind between intellectual activity and moral
response, through the place of moral judgement in guiding
conduct.   But I would like to suggest that there is a connection of a more intimate, though also perhaps more restricted
kind between the intellectual and the moral. (15)

At first sight, it might seem that ethical considerations
must be not just out of place but positively distorting if they
intrude upon critical assessment.   If we set aside properly
epistemic assessments such as true, false, valid, invalid,
probable, possible, relevant and so on, and allow to intrude
such notions as desirable and undesirable, or safe and
dangerous, then thought is corrupted by morality, in just the
same way as it might be by politics.   Thought has its own
autonomous standards, respect for which is constitutive of
intellectual autonomy.   And this is true even if it is moral
beliefs themselves which are being assessed.   If the question
is raised whether courage is always a virtue, or whether war
can ever be just, then autonomous standards will be appropriate to the arguments which ensue.

The matter takes on a different light, however, once we
realise that critical intellectual activity is only one possible
antecedent of belief.   There are many ways by which we
might come to think as we do about various things.   Our
belief may be no more than a casual impression that we have
picked up quite uncritically.   It may be something that we
have been told or taught but which we have never seriously
assessed.   It may have been instilled into us as an article of
faith.   It may have sprung from epistemically inappropriate
wishes and emotions as the ruling principle.   All of these
origins are alternatives to intellectual activity and only in a
weak sense are the resulting beliefs 'our own'.   They have
come to rest in our minds, as it were, or casually lodged
there, without the intervention of any process of critical discernment which would have integrated them or rejected them
in a way which made the resulting understanding in a much
stronger sense our own.

The possible ethical implication of all this, and the more
intimate sense in which the intellectual and the moral may be
related, arise from the fact that we are now clearly confronted
by a choice.   While only epistemic and not moral assessments
of belief are appropriate, nevertheless we have a choice
whether to engage in the epistemic scrutiny of our beliefs or
not.   We can choose whether to attach importance to intellectual activity as the source of our beliefs.   Something very
like a moral principle is present here, namely that, at least
on certain matters, we have a responsibility to determine the
truth as accurately as we can, proportioning our confidence
in it to the epistemic likelihood of its being true.

Not only is there a principle here, generative of an accom-
panying sense of responsibility, but there is also a whole set
of corresponding virtues.   These represent the outcomes of
struggles with adversaries both within and without us.   I
have in mind such virtues as justice, patience, humility, open-
mindedness, courage, integrity, readiness to submit to criticism and control of discordant passions.   In the event of our
failing to acquire these intellectual virtues, there is a whole
range of vices;   credulity, self-deception, precipitancy in
judgement, superstition, rationalisation, wishful thinking,
gullibility, prejudice and bigotry.

Intellectual education therefore would seem to imply yet a
third aspect additional to the two aspects already mentioned.
The first aspect that I mentioned was that of a range of cognitive content: the concepts, facts, principles, theories,
problems, interpretations and patterns of explanation and justification present in different fields.   The second aspect was
the activity of critical discernment in which we are alert for
falsehood, invalidity and inadequacy.   But now there emerges
a third aspect which is more like a development of moral character.   It involves a sense of responsibility towards intellectual standards, a fundamental principle and a whole range of
virtues.   For this reason, it might truly be said that the
intellectual disciplines are also ways of life.   They involve
not the passive gazing upon transparent truth, but struggles
with many kinds of adversary, not least within ourselves, on
the road to understanding.

VI

I have considered at some length the criticism that intellectual
education is altogether too exclusively one-sided because in
recent years this aspect of education has often been an object
of suspicion, if not of actual hostility.   Yet if we value the
development of autonomy as an ideal, the intellectual is one of
the main directions in which our educational institutions might

develop it.   No doubt an exclusive emphasis on intellect alone would be one-sided, though I have tried to show how even that, if done properly, would necessarily involve imagination, emotion and moral character to a much greater extent than might superficially be supposed.

It may well also be the case that, where the youngest children are concerned, child-centred suspicions of intellectual development are in place.   For intellectual education is not just a matter of acquiring knowledge or discovering facts, but involves critical thinking and the search for order, system and precision.   It requires concentrated study.   Something of these activities may be present in the earliest years of schooling, but the elements of abstractness and generality which they often involve may well require the learner to have voyaged some way on his Piagetian odyssey, or to have advanced some way through Whitehead's not dissimilar stages of romance, precision and generalisation.

Suspicions of intellectual education other than of a child-centred sort have also been expressed by egalitarians in recent years.   Intellectual education is divisive, not in the sense that it necessarily sets people against each other, but in the sense that it requires learners sooner or later to be divided according to their abilities, if the best possible progress is to be made by all.   Some educationists object to this, whether because it has implications for later status and income through its connections with the division of labour, or simply because it separates with apparent implications of better and worse now.   But intellectual education of certain sorts, and to the highest possible standards, is a fundamental requirement of the economy, and therefore even John Rawls would presumably think it justified as being to the ultimate advantage of all.   Quite apart from such instrumental justifications, however, there is surely a case to be made for giving an intellectual education to those who can profit from it simply as a worthwhile form of self-fulfilment.

A further point that I would like to make on intellectual education in relation to autonomy concerns a distinction between intellectual and personal autonomy.   Intellectual education is only one way through which autonomy can be developed, and even there other values must be involved if specific directions are to be chosen.   But there are many areas of autonomous judgement which call neither for great intellectual exercise, nor for initiation into great disciplines.   I have in mind areas to do with the relative minutiae of daily living. This more multiform version of autonomy is open to all and may be seen as the source of a dignity which all can possess. I have in mind the dignity which stems from being accorded, and from exercising, final responsibility as to the conduct of

one's life, both in respect of what to think and what to do.
A further point in deciding what to think about autonomy is
that the more it is successfully exercised, the stronger is the
sense in which each individual has a mind and an identity of
his own, though how fully he can enter into control of his
life will importantly depend on political and economic institutions and not just educational ones.

It has been argued by some people that autonomy is a somewhat self-referential notion. (16)   The whole concern of the
autonomous person is seen as being with forming his own
judgement according to his own criteria.   But this impression
derives, I think, from taking autonomy as the sole value,
whereas my own view would be that at least morality has
another root.   If we are concerned with education in a sense
wider than the moral, then many aspects of the curriculum
would need to be justified by reference to considerations
beyond autonomy.   If a person's concern were solely with a
judgement's being his own, then that requirement could be
fully met by a remarkably impoverished knowledge and understanding.

However, when coupled with a more ample conception of
education, autonomy has its point and enhances the overall
educational achievement.   This can be seen most clearly perhaps from an example.   Consider the pupil or student who
learns what has been said on some topic and who writes an
extended essay telling what all the authorities think and laying
them side by side.   The question remains: what does he
think himself?   Where is that activity of critical sifting in
which, at one and the same time, he moves towards a view as
to what is actually true, and also makes this knowledge his
own?   How has his understanding been enhanced as something integral to his life as a human being?

Perhaps autonomy is like happiness in this respect: that
you do not achieve it by making it your primary objective.
A decentred concern for appropriate standards would be the
primary point.   But the collateral effect on the person himself would be no less important for being indirect.

REFERENCES

1 R.F. Dearden (1968), 'The Philosophy of Primary Education' (London, Routledge & Kegan Paul).
2 R.F. Dearden (1972), Autonomy and Education, in R.F.
   Dearden, P.H. Hirst and R.S. Peters (eds), 'Education
   and the Development of Reason' (London, Routledge &
   Kegan Paul), ch. 25.
3 R.F. Dearden (1975), Autonomy as an Educational Ideal,

in S.C. Brown (ed.), 'Philosophers Discuss Education' (London, Macmillan), ch. 1.

4 For example, D.C. Phillips (1975), The Anatomy of Autonomy, in 'Educational Philosophy and Theory', vol. vii, no. 2.

5 F. Froebel (1826), 'The Education of Man', section 8.

6 A. Quinton (1971), Authority and Autonomy in Knowledge, in 'Proceedings of the Philosophy of Education Society', vol. v, no. 2, p. 208.

7 A.S. Neill (1967), 'Talking of Summerhill' (London, Gollancz), p. 133.

8 P.H. Hirst (1965), Liberal Education and the Nature of Knowledge, in R.D. Archambault (ed.), 'Philosophical Analysis and Education' (London, Routledge & Kegan Paul), pp. 116-21.

9 J. McPeck (1981), 'Critical Thinking and Education' (Oxford, Martin Robertson).

10 I have discussed this more fully in Controversial Issues and the Curriculum, in 'Journal of Curriculum Studies', vol. xiii, no. 1, 1981 (reprinted in this volume as chapter 7).

11 C. Dickens (1854), 'Hard Times', ch. 2.

12 J. Passmore (1980), 'The Philosophy of Teaching' (London, Duckworth), chs 8 and 9.

13 R.K. Elliott (1976), 'Imagination: a Kind of Magical Faculty', University of Birmingham, p. 14.

14 R. Hepburn (1966), Vision and Choice in Morality, in I.T. Ramsey (ed.), 'Christian Ethics and Contemporary Philosophy', SCM, p. 190.

15 I argued the following point more fully in Education and the Ethics of Belief, in 'British Journal of Educational Studies', vol. xxii, no. 1, 1974 (reprinted in this volume as chapter 8).

16 For example, E. Telfer in Autonomy as an Educational Ideal, in S.C. Brown (ed.), 'Philosophers Discuss Education' (1975, London, Macmillan), ch. 2.

10   THE ASSESSMENT OF LEARNING

Not one but many kinds of question can be raised about the
assessment of learning.   Yet as with learning itself so also
with assessment the topic has largely been left for the exclusive comment of psychologists.   Within the psychometric
tradition the most familiar questions raised have perhaps been
those concerned with the statistical treatment of the results of
tests and examinations.   Thus we are advised on both the
possibility and the desirability of weighting, converting, com-
bining and correlating scores.   Patterns of expected distribution are described and indeed prescribed.   Varying forms of
assessment are discussed with reference to such semi-technical
features as reliability and validity.

A more sociological perspective on assessment has served
recently to widen these discussions somewhat.   The wider
purposes and the intended and unintended consequences of
assessing learners have attracted interest even if that interest
has sometimes been of a rather doctrinaire kind showing how
we have here yet another evil prop to the capitalist system.
Not always quite so doctrinaire has been the interest in
accountability and in rational curriculum planning, both of
which themes have sharply raised questions about assessment.
And especially with the establishment of the Assessment of
Performance Unit a political aspect has become evident: he
who assesses may quickly become he who controls.

In now attempting a philosophical perspective I shall not
enter these debates on terms which have already been set.
I shall indeed make some passing comments on certain aspects
of the psychometric tradition and on certain purposes which
assessment serves.   But my principal interest will be to look
at assessment from an epistemological point of view.   The
results of any assessment of learning purport to be knowledge
of another human being.   Is such knowledge really possible?
In what sense can such claims be regarded as objective?   Is
self-assessment possible?   Can all learning be assessed, or is
there perhaps some which could not even in principle be
assessed?   Questions such as these require an epistemic
scrutiny which, to my knowledge, has not yet been attempted. (1)

Part three   Autonomy and learning

One of the very few philosophers to have had something to
say on these matters is Professor Flew, whose recent book
'Sociology, Equality and Education' devotes an interesting and
characteristically pugnacious chapter to Teaching and Testing. (2)   Flew's targets are people who think that assessment is a dispensable and even perhaps a pernicious adjunct
to teaching and learning.   Such a misguided view is vigor-
ously dismissed as implying 'insincerity of purpose' on the
part of a teacher.   For to be sincere in one's intention to
teach, he claims, implies a concern to know how far one's
intention is being achieved, though the particular form which
assessment ought to take is open to argument.

Flew is surely right about this, though the act of assessing,
as opposed to a 'concern to know', can hardly be *logically*
implied since there might on occasions be overriding ethical
reasons for refraining from such an act.   Also, it would be
quite untrue to say (and Flew does not say it) that there
cannot be any learning at all without assessment.   Much that
we all learn is never assessed either formally or informally.
For instance, as we go to work each day we learn a multitude
of trivia about the weather, people's habits, the joys and
vicissitudes of transport and the general state of our environment.   I may learn of a bargain in some store and in my
excitement step under a bus, thus precluding even the possibility of assessment.   There may be a minimal sense in which
what we thus learn is always assessed, for example for its
truth, consistency or agreeableness, but this is different
from assessing whether we have learned it.

Assessment is necessary not for learning to occur but for
us to know that it has occurred, and an intelligent teacher
will wish to know that for all sorts of purposes.   Above all
he will wish to know it for the intelligent execution of his
task.   Assessment provides him with the feedback on progress in learning necessary to determine the best manner,
sequence, direction, pace and level of difficulty in his teaching.   The purposes of such 'formative' assessment are, as
Flew argues, those which are most unavoidable since they are
internal to the intention to teach in a way that 'summative'
assessment, coming at the end and serving such purposes as
those of comparison and selection, is not unavoidable, though
it may often be desirable.

II

For us to know that there has been learning, the learned capacity must be evidenced in a way that may broadly be described as behavioural, though without any theoretical commitment
to behaviourism in saying that.   That is to say, the learned

capacity must be evidenced in some appropriate performance, such as saying, writing, making, demonstrating or showing. Some such link must exist in order to tie our claim to know to the reality which we claim to know something about. Usually, of course, there is a separable product which can be studied or shown to others at leisure. Even where a performance is itself the product, as in swimming, playing the violin, speaking French or acting, a more permanent record can in principle be made by means of film or tape. The frequent practical desirability of having such a product for the purposes of assessment is surely one important reason why schools so often ask for a piece of writing where in real life speech would suffice. Similarly, teachers of very young children hear them read aloud though as adults they will be expected to read silently. It is the purposes of assessment rather than any intended representativeness of real life which justify this.

The product has to be judged true or false, good or bad, but that judgement then serves as the basis of an inference to learned capacity, and unlike the MOT test with cars the inference is to a relatively permanent capacity. The case is quite different where the product is presented not as the result of a learning exercise but as a contribution to the advancement of learning in the sense of the stock of human knowledge. The work done for a research degree presents both of these aspects: from it we infer something of what the student has learned, but it may also be viewed more impersonally as a contribution to knowledge, a new inhabitant of the Popperian third world as it were. (3)

This capacity which we infer could be present in a group, as it may be when the product judged is a collective frieze or a geographical land use map of a district. In that case it would be to commit the fallacy of division to attribute to each member of the group what the group as a whole may truly be said to have learned to do. This particular child may simply have stuck in the pictures or done the red bits. For this reason, teachers anxious that all in the group should individually have learned what there is to learn will draw together a group project towards its end for a sharing by each in what has been learned by the group. It is in fact often not very valuable to know that a learned capacity inheres in a group, for the simple reason that the existence of groups is apt to be transient. Yet an individual's learned capacity to co-operate within a group may survive the group's dissolution and have some value. However, I shall assume that it is the learning of individuals which is to be assessed.

An individual's learned capacities are *evidenced* in his behaviour. But that is not of course to say that the learning

just is the performance.   The gap between learned capacity
and behavioural evidence can be insisted upon by drawing
attention to the ambiguity which attaches to just what is being
evidenced. (4)   Practical and physical skills are relatively
unambiguous in this respect.   This is because these capacities are actually specified by reference to classes of overt
performances.   If the learner swims two lengths of the baths,
or if the carpenter constructs a table incorporating numerous
dovetail joints, then we are fairly safe in attributing to him
learned capacities to swim and to make such joints.   The inference is particularly free from hazards when success is
achieved, though even then the performance may, though im-
plausibly, have been that of his identical twin brother, or
have been an extraordinary succession of fluke cuts with the
chisel.   Again, he might not have acquired the skill but have
possessed it from birth in the swimming example, or he may
have learned it but not from us, contrary to what we had been
assuming.   If he fails, however, the inference is more hazar-
dous, for then he may have the capacity but simply have
failed to understand the instructions, or have lacked motivation, or have been in some way temporarily disabled.

Such inferential hazards might reasonably be said to be
theoretically possible but practically negligible.   But that is
much less true in the case of what might broadly be called
intellectual learning, or the acquisition of beliefs, knowledge-
that, and understanding.   This is because what the learner
is said to believe, know or understand is specified by reference not to a class of overt performance but by reference to
propositions.   And not only can the same propositional attitude be behaviourally evidence in a great variety of ways but
also the same behavioural 'evidence' can fit a great variety of
propositional attitudes.   For example, a moral belief that one
should do the best one can for one's parents may be evidenced
in different societies in quite opposite behaviours, such as
killing in one and nursing in another.   Contrariwise, a scientist's experimental behaviour may reflect either his belief, or
his disbelief, or his doubt concerning a hypothesis under test.

To take a concrete classroom case, what are we to infer
from a child's writing down 21 as the answer to the question
of the sum of the numbers from 1 to 6?   He may have suc-
cessively added the numbers, applied a mechanical rule,
arrived by insight at a rule, copied the answer, guessed it or
by chance happened to get it right in following a quite wrong
procedure.   With students and with more complex products
further hazards are present.   Students may insincerely say
that they think what they suppose the teacher to want them
to think.   They may arrange for substitute examinees.
They may misunderstand the task, or even deliberately do
badly, as might happen with assessment for some military

purpose.   Our sample of questions may have been peculiarly
lucky for them.   The induction to relative permanence may
be fallaciously based on what is in fact an ephemeral effect of
last-minute revision.   Originality may be attributed to them
when in fact their views reflect the unpublished thoughts of
their teachers.   And so on....

And in all of this we are assuming that the assessor is
doing his job properly, whereas he may misperceive, be care-
less in his recording, or be incompetent to judge (possibly as
a result of an 'economy measure' which has made him judge
too much in an attempt to cut down on the numbers of exami-
ners).   Again, the circumstances of the assessment may have
been such as unfairly to rush, or assess too soon, or when
unfit, or in an unfamiliar form or setting.   These possibilities
serve to remind us of the fact that assessing learners is not
merely attempting to find out something true about them.   It
ought also at the same time to be an endeavour to do justice
to them.   Wrongly to assess a person is not simply to make a
mistake but, particularly if he is underrated, also to do him
an injustice.   For what we learn in this way constitutes part
of our estimate of another human being.   It is part of the
basis of his reputation.

This lengthy and far from complete list of inferential hazards
where intellectual assessment is concerned may in practice be
less worrying than it at first seems.   Measures can be adopted to counter the principal perils.   Examples can be suitably
varied, deception anticipated, allowances made for various contingencies and so on.   Very high in importance amongst such
measures will be the choice of an appropriate form of assessment.   Suppose, for example, that we wish to determine
whether someone has correctly learned that Ulster was once
covered by ice.   What form should our assessment take?   A
sentence completion exercise, or selection from a multiple
choice, might signify nothing more than the recall of rote
learning, or even a guess.   So we may explore in addition
his capacity to draw ecological consequences and hence see if
he actually understands what it concretely means for a land
surface to be covered by ice.   But still it might be asked
whether he actually *knows* this, which might require his being
able appropriately to ground his beliefs.   That would lead us
into assessing his awareness of the evidence for Ulster's
having been covered by ice.   In determining the appropriate
form of assessment, there is thus a logical priority to be
attached to determining exactly what it is that we wish to
assess.   Without that prior determination very little can be
said about the form which assessment should take.   As with
teaching generally, becoming clearer as to what we are trying
to do is logically prior to deciding how best to do it.

III

Is certainty ever possible in claiming to know that someone
has learned something?   If by 'certainty' is meant that there
is no logical possibility of error, then certainty is no more
possible here than it is in other non-mathematical fields of
knowledge.   The inferential gap between behavioural evidence or product on the one hand and learned capacity on the
other cannot be crossed with complete logical security, and
attributing relative permanence to the capacity involves the
further hazards of induction.   But in practice many of the
hazards which do preclude logical certainty can be rendered
less likely by being guarded against in various ways.   General scepticism as regards this whole field of judgements seems
no more warranted than it does in many other fields.   And,
as with sceptics elsewhere, here too they can be seen to be
inconsistently relying on some other correct assessment in
assembling evidence of incorrectness in a particular case.
That is to say, to claim that an attempt at assessment has
failed is just as much a claim to knowledge as is the claim to
have succeeded.   If I point out that it was an error to attribute insight to a pupil because in fact he had only guessed at
the answer and accidentally got it right, then I claim actually
to know *that*.

There is such a thing as 'the state of the art', embodying
measures and practices so far evolved that have been found to
be necessary and beneficial for accurate assessment.   As
with other fields of knowledge this too will be an historically
developed possession which needs to be passed on to each
fresh entry to the teaching profession and from time to time
revised and developed further.   By a conscientious application of this art, at least relative certainty may be attained.
That is to say, we may have every good reason to attribute a
certain learned capacity to someone and know of no good
reason to withhold that attribution.   But the sceptic's reminder that relative certainty is not absolute certainty leaves
open the logical space necessary to accommodate the errors
which from time to time will undoubtedly occur.

But narrowing the scope for possible error is not the only
consideration.   As forms of assessment become more sophisticated in this respect, so also do they normally become more
costly in time and materials.   Whether the additional costs
incurred in a nearer approach to certainty will be justified
will depend on the purpose of the assessment.   Determining
whether someone is ready to proceed to the next page, with
ample opportunity for immediate correction if in error, is
plainly quite a different matter from determining whether a
professionally important public qualification or licence is to be
awarded.   There are thus at least three major considerations

relevant to appraising an attempt to assess learned capacities:
the truth of the knowledge claim, justice to the person assessed, and the overall utility of the exercise, that is to say its
various costs in relation to its usefulness and importance.

IV

In taking the truth of the knowledge claim as the first of
these major considerations I am of course assuming objectivity
to be possible in assessing.   But in the literature of the
psychometric tradition the term 'objective' is usually confined
to tests where the answers are so straightforward and uncontroversial as to permit of mechanical marking: 'mechanical'
either in making undemanding calls on the markers' judgement
or in literally being done by a machine.   Even so, such a
mechanical procedure frequently rests on false assumptions.
Supposedly 'objective' items, such as odd-man-out, shared
properties, or multiple choice alternatives have often been
discovered to be more controversial than the test constructor
had supposed.   And such forms of assessment are rightly
seen as grossly inappropriate in form for detecting many
learned capacities.   To take an extreme example, a philosophy
test could be of this 'objective' kind if it asked for the correct spelling of the author of 'Beyond Good and Evil' but it
would be quite unable to elicit the student's own considered
response to Nietzsche's critique of Christian morality.

But why should it be granted that such mechanically mark-
able tests are alone to be regarded as 'objective'?   Must it be
conceded that as soon as skilled judgement is called for then
objectivity retreats from the scene?   Certainly all but the
simplest forms of assessment do call for skilled judgement in
the assessor.   And in such judgement a high degree of
agreement may nevertheless still be achievable.   Does this
agreement show that such judgement is objective?

People used erroneously to agree that the thing to do in a
plague was to gather together in church and pray, thus unfortunately spreading the plague that much faster.   Juries
may agree on a man's guilt and yet be wrong in their verdict.
Contrariwise, a man may disagree with others and yet be
right.   Apparently in the early stages of the Watergate inves-
tigations the newspaper reporters involved were virtually
alone in their opinion that there was a scandal to be uncover-
ed.   Similarly, a doctor may disagree with colleagues over a
diagnosis and yet be proved right, though with small benefit
if that is at the post-mortem.   Yet if what we think true is
in fact true, then we will agree, since truth is a consistent
whole.   But that is to see agreement as the consequence of
true belief rather than the criterion of it.

If an assessment is to be objective, then there must really
be present or absent the learned capacity that is the subject
of inference from the product or performance.   Granted the
criteria determining what we ought to be looking for (which
have equally to be granted in mechanical 'objective' tests)
then in principle and indeed often in practice there is no
reason that objective judgement should not be expected.   If
assessors disagree then they should look again, for example
they should reread the script or check their records or seek
further samples of work.   With complex achievements, however, there may be some disagreement over the criteria as to
what counts or, more likely, disagreement over their relative
importance.   Then the economics of assessment and the politics of compromise typically come into play, and an agreed
assessment is negotiated rather than discovered.   The practical need to come to a decision in a limited time rules out the
protracted delay, even perhaps the interminable delay, that
full agreement would require.   The claims of truth have to
be weighed here against the utility of the exercise.   But in,
for example, averaging divergent assessments the truth is not
entirely lost from sight.   Rather it is located with less precision.

Yet there is a so far unmentioned way in which agreement
does have an epistemic bearing on the possibility of objective
judgement.   It must indeed be granted that one assessor may
be right and the others wrong, as with the clever doctor's
diagnosis.   Just conceivably, someone might always be right
though nobody else agrees with him.   A man might in fact be
a superb mathematician whose rapidity of insight and brevity
of demonstration leave everyone else bewildered at the start
and never able to retrace the path of his reasoning.   But if
we are to have grounds for regarding someone as a skilled
assessor then we must at least come to agree with the general
run of his judgements.   Whatever is in fact the case, if we
are to *know* that he is a skilled judge then we must be able to
follow him to agreed conclusions.   This again is not to say
that truth consists in agreement, but that agreement with a
person's judgements is a condition of our being able to regard
him as a skilled judge.

This epistemic as opposed to practical necessity of agreement
can easily be made to look (for example by sociologists of
knowledge) as though assessors are selected merely for their
orthodoxy.   But while a certain orthodoxy may be present as
to which criteria are important, it nevertheless remains an
objective matter whether or not the criterial features so valued
are present or absent in the person judged.   The question of
the rightness of the choice of criteria, however, raises subtle
and fascinating questions as to who is to be regarded as an
authority on a subject and on what grounds: questions which

would deserve the fullest of separate treatment in their own
right.

V

In the light of this discussion of objectivity in assessment,
what can be made of the notion of self-assessment?   Do not
the points made about the relation of truth to agreement rule
out self-assessment?   I do not think so.   By 'self-assessment' of course one means more than simply that a learner
should keep a record of the work that he has completed, for
example the books that he has read.   There must be judgement of his work as correct or incorrect, good or bad.   Yet
there is an evident absurdity in the idea of a child's hearing
himself read, or the idea of his considering how confident he
feels that he has understood as an objective test.   There is
no possibility of correction from such directions as these,
and hence no ground for the distinction between 'really is'
and 'seems to me'.

But the case is rather different where a child checks his
own performance against a tape or answer book, or where he
consults a reference work as a check, or where he uses
'self-correcting apparatus' such as Montessori's.   In cases
such as these there is the possibility of correction and so of
the training in objective judgement which might eventually
produce a competent self-assessor.   Yet the distinction
between self-correction and other-correction cannot be sharp,
as one can see from the case of the child who checks his
addition sum by the reverse subtraction of an addend from
the addition answer, or who checks a division sum by multi-
plying quotient and divisor.   Self-assessment will be simplest
where a straightforward comparison in terms of identity is
possible between what has been done and the correct answer,
as in mechanical 'objective' tests.   With sophisticated capacities and their complex and individual products, such as
essays, the possibilities of self-assessment in learning are
much more limited since comparison in terms of identity is not
possible and skilled judgement is needed.   'Model answers'
may have some pedagogic uses here but cannot suffice if justice is to be done to an individual and non-standard product.

VI

A curious but popular development of recent years in some
schools has been to produce assessments not of products but
of the 'effort' that went into producing them.   No doubt all
teachers welcome and wish to encourage effort of this kind
but when it is regarded as an alternative object of assessment

the context is usually one in which ordinary learning achievements are so tiny, or even non-existent, that effort is virtually all there is to assess.   As with awarding certificates for
100 per cent attendance at school, so here the thought is to
give a fillip to the battered self-esteem of the less able.
Thus they too can receive high grades and even be awarded
prizes.   More to the point for some minds is the consideration that employers looking for unskilled labour do attach
selective advantages to applicants whose qualities of character
if not their intellects have something relevant to offer.   It is
not that the Kantian will may shine like a jewel though it
accomplish nothing in results, but that effort will indeed
accomplish something of the sort that these employers have in
mind.   Why, then, are more appropriate learning tasks not
chosen for these pupils while they are at school?   If that
were done, then learning and not just fruitless effort would
result and the indignity of the consolation prize could be
avoided.   One of the root difficulties here seems to be a
strong attachment to comparative or 'norm-referenced' assessment.

One sort of comparative assessment is that in which a pre-
conceived pattern of mark distribution is imposed on a set of
scores.   Thus, for example, only 5 per cent may be allowed
an 'A' mark and a similar percentage must have 'E's.   There
are some epistemological puzzles about this.   How is it known
in advance that there will be this pattern?   Reference will be
made to what in the past has been *found* with certain characteristics in certain populations.   But while that may warrant
a rational prediction, it cannot without committing the naturalistic fallacy justify the normative requirement that a future
array of results be *prescribed* the expected pattern.   Not
only is this fallacious but it also runs counter to the non-ideo-
logical convictions of assessors who know from their experience
that the distribution of results will vary in its skew from
group to group and from year to year.   No doubt standards
can drift but that does nothing to warrant distributional pre-
scriptions.

Furthermore, prescriptive distribution is involved in difficulties similar to those of the coherence theory of truth (at
least in one interpretation of that theory).   For just as a
fully coherent set of propositions may yet be false (as by
definition is the case with a well written work of fiction), so
too might a prescriptive distribution indicate much or very
little about the positive achievements that are present.   A
score of 10 per cent might warrant an 'A' or a score of 90
per cent an 'E' on distributional grounds.   Rather similarly,
in the army the last man out would be put on fatigues no
matter how fast he was.   *Some* connection with the reality of
achievement has to be retained for there to be an array to

distribute, but it could be a very slender connection indeed.

Comparative assessment effected by prescriptive distribution also invites competition, a precondition of which is scarcity of some desired good, for example 'A' marks. But learning achievements are infinitely repeatable. No natural scarcity can apply to them. They are limited only by such things as variations in educability and scarcity of access to limited educational resources, for example places in certain institutions or expensive equipment. Prescriptive distribution therefore introduces an entirely artificial scarcity and competition into the activity of learning. This may in some circumstances be justified, for example if a limited number and therefore perhaps the best of a group are to be selected for something. But much of classroom learning, it may be argued, ought not in any direct way to be concerned with selection but rather with achieving the maximum development of desirable learning potential for each individual.

A second sort of comparative assessment might nevertheless still prevail. This would be so quite apart from any prescriptive distribution if the same uniform standard were to be applied across a whole group. In principle there would be nothing competitive in that since all might achieve the same marks and there is no artificially introduced scarcity of grades. In practice self-esteem will be enhanced or chastened by comparison and even a quite praiseworthy degree of positive achievement is likely to be transformed into something negatively perceived as failure, for example as being the lowest or worst mark in the class.

Sensitive to what I think is rightly perceived as potential injustice to positive achievement here, many teachers now attempt by means of small group or even individual work to assess learning by standards related to the estimated potential of the individual himself. The ethical intent behind this rejection of comparative assessment nevertheless needs comment. In the first place, and as things are, there inevitably comes a form of terminal comparative assessment when pupils or students face a job market concerned to select the best from those on offer for some work. But there is no valid inference from this feature of the division of labour in society to the conclusion that such selection-orientated comparative assessment must be the norm throughout schooling. Even from a viewpoint confined solely to employment considerations the best preparation by the school for the job market may still be to develop each individual's potential by tasks and standards tailored to him personally.

Another comment of a more epistemological character is relevant. Whence are derived these individually tailored

standards?   How can we frame our expectations as to what in
a given field of learning is possible for a pupil?   It may be
that a notion of 'normal' degrees of difficulty and rates of
progress is an essential conception presupposed by any individualised adaptation to particular learners.   It seems to me
that the ethical intentions behind the rejection of comparative
assessment must recognise this point as a condition of giving
a coherent account of how individualised programmes can be
devised.   The tasks of learning themselves imply nothing
about individual differences.   The presumption in the face of
such tasks must therefore be that all can cope with them.
The reality of human differences will typically falsify this presumption but it would seem to imply that the first assessments
should be in terms of a common standard, for example a given
standard of linguistic and reading ability.   Experience of differences in subsequent progress can then be taken as a guide
to sensitive individual tailoring.

But there will remain an epistemic connection between individual and comparative standards, and between individual and
humanly possible patterns of progress.   Thus the teacher
will judge each child's work by reference to what it is appropriate to expect from that child, but those very expectations
can only be framed by a teacher whose notions of the possible
have emerged from comparisons.   For this reason new teachers, with little comparative awareness in detail of what is
possible, have an understandable difficulty in framing just
expectations.   And since truth may be as desirable in self-
concepts as it is elsewhere there is some reason not to conceal
differences from individuals themselves.   Children are in any
case shrewd enough to notice them.   But on the other hand
it seems ethically indefensible to deny appropriate success and
satisfaction by continuing to set inappropriate common tasks
and by persisting in applying inappropriate common standards.

VII

So far I have made no comment on the common and important
distinction between formal and informal assessment.   By
'formal' assessment I refer to those situations in which the
person assessed undergoes set-piece testing or examination in
the understood role of examinee.   By 'informal' assessment I
refer to the process of feedback which is, or ought to be, a
continuous part of teaching and learning.   There cannot be
too much informal assessment, one is tempted to say.   In my
opening references to Flew it was argued that such assessment
is a requirement of practical rationality in deliberate teaching
and learning: to will the end is to will the means, part of
which is monitoring how you are doing as a condition of intelligent choice and variation.   Such informal assessment is

aptly called 'formative' in the literature, by contrast with the 'summative' or end-summary character of formal assessment.

The point of making this admittedly rough-and-ready distinction goes beyond questions of practical utility, or the desirability of forming a discriminating response to changing attitudes towards assessment.   For may it not be the case that some learning objectives, perhaps even some of the highest importance, can be assessed only informally?   I have in mind certain desirable attitudes in the learner towards both the process and the content of learning.   Teachers seek interest in learning and seriousness about it, heightened levels of aspiration, certain sorts of genuinely felt response to content and shifts towards more desirable bases of self-esteem.   How is the acquisition of attitudes such as these to be assessed?   It can certainly be done and if necessary recorded informally, though with sophisticated students even informal assessment here can be compromised by clever image-management.   But it seems clear that such attitudes cannot be formally assessed, for the following reasons.

A formal assessment situation is by definition one in which qualities and capacities are deliberately displayed for judge-mental scrutiny.   But this means that the motivation at work is at variance with that appropriate to a display of the attitudes in question.   Sincerity is compromised.   The examinee's motive is, rightly, self-display, but so to display these attitudes would be merely to act as if they were one's attitudes.   Sincere manifestations of these educationally desirable attitudes are possible only in their natural settings, where they can indeed be informally and unobtrusively observed.   There is an obvious difference between displaying what are taken to be the expected attitudes and their natural and unself-conscious manifestation because they are one's attitudes.

A painful dilemma may thus confront a teacher who has liberal educational objectives in mind: either he formally examines those attitudes, in which case he invites insincerity, or he does not, in which case they are likely to suffer the devaluation consequent upon being non-examined.   They may be made to seem frills which the hard-nosed cannot even regard as real.   There are apparently those who are able to recognise learning only when the results are couched in formally quantified terms, and they may currently be gaining in political influence both inside and outside schools.   How, then, do you praise music to the tone-deaf?

VIII

My general endeavour in this article has been to widen the
discussion of assessment beyond the concerns of the psycho-
metricians and more recently the sociologists.   Of course
there is nothing new in pointing out the fallibility of assessment procedures, but I have attempted a more systematic
epistemological perspective on these familiar facts.   Starting
from the admission that we must have behavioural evidence of
learning, I then related that point to some wider issues of
behaviourism and the inherent ambiguity of behaviour, especially where intellectual learning is concerned.   But besides
truth, justice and utility have also to be taken into account.

I argued that it was an unwarranted restriction to see
objectivity as confined to so-called 'objective' tests, since all
assessment should aim to discover what is really there and in
that sense aims to be objective.   At least relative certainty
is achievable and while agreement in judgements is not necessarily truth, neither is it necessarily mere orthodoxy.   Self-
assessment was argued to be possible, provided there was
room for correction if in error and especially where a comparison in terms of identity is the test.

The assessment of effort was seen to be a symptom of a
certain deeper unease about making comparative judgements.
Such comparisons might involve fallacious distributional pre-
scriptions or engender some unwanted consequences of competition.   But even if we confine our judgements to individuals
as such, and not as members of groups, still there is an
implicit comparison in framing standards of what to expect.

Finally, I argued that not all learning, and not some of the
most educationally valuable learning, can be formally assessed,
which poses a difficult dilemma in a harsh political climate
which insists on the formally quantifiable as being alone real
or worthwhile.

REFERENCES

1 I am grateful for their comments on early drafts of this
   article to Ieuan Lloyd, Terence Moore, Brian Price and
   Robert Wood.
2 A. Flew (1976), 'Sociology, Equality and Education'
   (London, Macmillan), ch. 6.
3 I refer of course to the distinction between the three
   worlds of (roughly) physical objects, conscious states and
   cultural products made by K.R. Popper in his 'Objective
   Knowledge' (1972, Oxford, Clarendon).
4 I have discussed this point more fully in my book 'Prob-

lems in Primary Education' (1976, London, Routledge &
Kegan Paul), ch. 2.

11 BEHAVIOUR MODIFICATION: TOWARDS AN ETHICAL APPRAISAL

Behaviour modification can be appraised from many different points of view. We could consider its efficiency by comparison with other ways of attempting to change behaviour, or we could consider the training programme that it implies, or we could look into its cost-effectiveness, or, as in the present case, we could attempt an ethical appraisal of it. But each of these and indeed other approaches take it for granted that behaviour modification of the kind envisaged is at any rate possible. But is it? The possibility in question here is not technical, financial, legal or administrative but conceptual. And the heart of the matter is the particular concept of 'behaviour' which is presupposed in these programmes of modification. Certainly an ethical appraisal of behaviour modification, if it is to have any philosophical validity, must first undertake a preliminary scrutiny of just what it is that it is proposed to modify. Confusion on this point may well be one of the principal obstacles to a wider acceptance of behaviour modification in education.

According to B.F. Skinner, from whom behaviour modifiers generally acknowledge taking their inspiration, 'mental life and the world in which it is lived are inventions.' (1) It is just this kind of detachment of physical behaviour from a mental world of belief, desire, trying, imagination, experience, attention and in general of understanding that makes so necessary a preliminary inquiry into the concept of behaviour that is being taken for granted. Of course, it may immediately be said that the existence of such 'mentalistic' features is not denied. What is denied is that they have any important explanatory significance, or that they make much difference to behaviour. Yet from an ethical point of view the presence or absence of certain beliefs, desires or intentions makes a very great difference indeed. Legally, it could make the difference between whether you went to prison or not.

In the first place, it is clear that the same 'behavioural topography' can carry importantly different and even incompatible mentalistic descriptions. For example, suppose that someone's observable movements are to drive along a stretch of road at fifty miles an hour. What is he doing? He may be carefully observing or deliberately breaking a speed limit. He may be escaping from a crime or going to help someone.

He may be thoughtfully conserving petrol or callously disre-
garding the victim of an accident.   These fuller stories are
of great ethical and also of legal significance.   The different
versions do not all come to the same thing.

It may be said that these differences can be accommodated
by the behaviourist simply by looking at the driver's subsequent behaviour, when different topographies will emerge.
But which of the descriptions is true is already an objective
matter of fact regardless of what the driver does subsequently.   If in the next moment a meteorite fell on him and thus
precluded any subsequent observations, the alternative mentalistic descriptions would nevertheless still each carry an
objective truth-value (true or false).   How we can find out
whether something is true is a different question from what it
is for it to be true.

My point is that there is more to behaviour than its topographical configuration.   No doubt Skinner would try to meet
this point by saying that the same 'topography' (his term) can
be controlled by different contingencies of reinforcement.
Thus a rat may press a lever on two occasions (same topography) though in the one case to obtain food when hungry
and in the other case to obtain water when thirsty. (2)   Differences of 'meaning' can therefore be accommodated without
reference to anything so mysterious and elusive as mind.

While some critics would take Skinner to task here for supposing there to be a close analogy between rats and people,
ethologists might very well wish to question whether justice
has been done even to rats.   What is the force of the phrase
'to obtain' food or water, for example.   Attempting to cope
with the important differences which there can be in behaviour which is topographically the same by referring to different contingencies or reinforcement shifts the problem elsewhere, but it does not solve it.   Mentalistic explanations
will reappear if we ask how environmental features can mean
anything to us, how they can be selectively attended to and
can be intelligently connected with what they are supposed to
reinforce.

To approach the same difficulty from the opposite direction,
consider what it means for two people to do the same thing.
Initial plausibility may be given to a behaviourist account of
this sameness if we pick some such example as a child copying
a teacher writing the letter 'a', for here there is an obvious
topographical likeness.   But take another case.   Headteachers are often currently worried by the falling number of children on their school rolls.   Two headteachers might 'do the
same thing' in that they both actively set about making their
schools more secure in this respect.   Yet one of them does

this by issuing to parents what he hopes is an attractive
prospectus, while the other opens a nursery class.   Where
two pieces of behaviour are as topographically different as
these are, reference must be made to the guiding intentions
to bring out the important respects in which the behaviour is
the same.   Thus whether we consider how topographically
very different behaviour can yet be the same (the headteachers), or whether we consider how behaviour which is
topographically the same can yet be very different (the
drivers), either way reference needs to be made to 'mentalistic' features if the behaviour is to be at all adequately characterised.

An absurd consequence of ignoring the understanding which
accompanies and indeed importantly constitutes human behaviour is evident in Poteet's purportedly 'clever and useful'
definition of 'out-of-seat behaviour'.   Backed by references
to suitable authorities, he defines this posterior irregularity
as follows: 'the seat portion of the child's body is not in
contact with any portion of the seat of the child's chair.' (3)
The educational context, of course, is that of children improp-
erly leaving their work to wander round the classroom.   But
in that context the behavioural definition is absurd.   The
spatial location of the child's bottom is not the point.   If the
child gets up to sharpen a pencil, or to pick up something
fallen, or to show respect to a visitor, or to leave the room
with permission, then all is well.   It is only out-of-seat
behaviour which the child knows to be in breach of a classroom rule that needs to be 'modified'.   Only absurdity results
from trying to dispense with the child's own recognition of
what is appropriate behaviour. (4)

Similar absurdities follow from misconceived attempts to
specify regular laws of behaviour modification.   For example,
if a child becomes a nuisance by putting up his hand to
answer a question when he does not in fact know the answer,
it may sometimes be good advice simply to ignore his hand.
But this cannot be some sort of law, since on a particular
occasion it may be far more effective to hear the ridiculous
answer safe in the knowledge that its reception by the rest of
the class will be a strong discouragement to that child for the
future.   Again, it may be useful to praise a child in such a
way that he may serve as a model, but on a particular occasion this may be so counter-productive as merely to embarrass
the praised child and to produce detestation rather than model-
ling in the others.   How behaviour is understood makes a
very great difference indeed.

Consider next the nature of the connection between the
occurrence of some reinforcing environmental contingency and
the behaviour which it is to reinforce.   How is that connec-

in much the same way as they live generally (aggressively, considerately, competitively, impulsively, cautiously, etc.) so too will the perspective from which behaviour modification is viewed reflect the modifier himself. He may be a person of broad humanitarian sympathies or perhaps, at the other extreme, a human cripple who would quite naturally think of personal relationships in terms of mechanical engineering or animal training. And the ambiguity in the notion of 'behaviour' which runs right through behaviour modification can mislead people of very different perspectives here into supposing that they are all really part of one and the same movement. The case is quite parallel to the apparent, but only apparent, sameness of principle as between the political left and right regarding 'equality of educational opportunity'.

Suppose that a more 'mentalistic' concept of behaviour is adopted and reference to beliefs, desires, intentions, experience and understanding is allowed to be in order, how might an ethical appraisal of behaviour modification proceed then? One obvious form which it might take is to look at the ends which the various techniques are used to serve. Skinner, for example, is openly hostile to the central liberal value of autonomy, though he grossly misunderstands it. In place of autonomy we are offered survival. But then it would be the manner of the surviving which mattered, and if we turned to 'Walden Two' for a fuller and more detailed picture of what was intended, we should find a simple hedonism in which everyone gets what he wants because the behaviour managers have adjusted wants to what people are in fact going to get. (10) Skinner calls that condition one of freedom and happiness.

One way in which Skinner fudges the issue is by pretending that the controllers are as much affected as are the controlled: 'the relation between controller and controlled is reciprocal.' (11) The grain of truth in this is that in any project there will be objective conditions for success to which the agent has to submit. For example, you cannot travel from A to B without taking time and using energy, no matter how powerful you are. But there is also the question of who gets what he wants, whose is the initiative and whose intentions are being carried out. Generally speaking, behaviour modifiers in education have addressed themselves to teachers in their dealings with children. Would it make no difference if instead they addressed themselves to administrators at local or national level in their dealings with teachers?

It would be thoroughly in keeping with the 'technology' power fantasy for behaviour modifiers to express dismissive impatience with the problems of choosing and balancing educational ends. But if ends do conflict, as indeed they do, then

there is no alternative to the exercise of judgement in balancing one against another.   Such questions will regularly need
to be asked as whether an adequate range of ends is envisaged, whose interest is at stake, and how far consent is
necessary.

If justifiable ends are being pursued, is it then simply a
matter of choosing the most effective means, in which case the
behaviour modifier's preoccupation with technique might be
given full play?   Not quite, for ends may not justify means.
If we have good political ends, may we use torture and terror-
ism to achieve them?   If we have good educational ends, may
we use electroconvulsive shock, bellow down a megaphone at a
child standing next to us, medicate perhaps a million 'hyper-
active' children, or subject someone to a programme of sustained and vicious verbal abuse, to choose four actual examples
from the field?

There is an ethical debate here between those who think that
certain values must be adhered to regardless of the consequences and those who think that circumstances and consequences may justify exceptions to otherwise binding principles.
The position which one takes concerning objectionable means to
good ends will therefore reflect an option and not a necessity.
However, there are two general points which can perhaps be
validly made about means and ends in behaviour modification
programmes.

First, in education the means that may be chosen are typically constrained by the ends pursued.   If a certain kind of
understanding is aimed at, then the means chosen must be
compatible with the emergence of such an end-state.   This is
why a theory of cognitive learning must be importantly determined at least in part by the nature of the subject matter or
topic to be learned. (12)   The 'reinforcers' typically envisaged are extrinsic to such ends and therefore at best what we
will then be offered is a theory that explains how you can
motivate learning but not what (cognitive) learning is.   But
second, it is not entirely satisfactory to concentrate on extrinsic motivation if we are concerned to educate.   Behaviour
modifiers do sometimes recognise this and speak of a transition
from extrinsic to intrinsic motivation when the stage-managed
reinforcers are withdrawn.   But the nature of this transition
is invariably left thoroughly obscure, probably because it
would reintroduce such despised 'mentalistic' concepts as satisfaction, enjoyment, pleasure, and a sense of mastery. (13)

Whether the concern is with ends or means, a major presupposition in both cases would be that it is the child who has to
change, and that presupposition may in particular circumstances be quite unjustified.   What is really called for may be a

political fight for more resources, or changes in the teachers, or a review of the curriculum or an institutional reorganisation.   In this way, behaviour modification programmes may be as open to criticism as are some forms of pastoral care for being strategies of defensive conservatism and hence politically biased or ideologically committed.   Certainly it is to over-sell behaviour modification to present it as the single answer to all of the educational ills that have caught the headlines in recent years.

In conclusion, I would like to identify some features of merit in the behaviour modification movement.   My primary criticism has been the philosophically familiar one that there is a central and damaging confusion over what 'behaviour' is. I have also suggested that more specific criticisms should distinguish between essential deficiencies of the theory and contingent deficiencies of a particular behaviour modifier as a person.   But together with these deficiencies come some things of value too.   There are some pertinent criticisms of traditional approaches to motivation, such as that reinforcement is characteristically too exclusively negative, too infrequent and often too long delayed, as when a few negative criticisms are all that is to be found on an essay returned six months after it was handed in.   Furthermore, this movement is helping to restore classroom management to a place of proper importance in teacher training.   And frustrated or demoralised teachers who face nothing but disruption and non-cooperation in their classes are at least being made to feel that someone has seen their plight and cares.   In that last sad situation, it nevertheless has to be said that some care still needs to be exercised in choosing one's friends.

REFERENCES

1 B.F. Skinner (1974), 'About Behaviourism' (London, Cape), p. 104.
2 Ibid., p. 90.
3 J.A. Poteet (1973), 'Behaviour Modification' (ULP), p. 7. I am indebted to my colleague Dr D.I. Lloyd for drawing my attention to this example.
4 P.S. Wilson elaborates on this point in his book 'Interest and Discipline in Education' (1971, Routledge & Kegan Paul), p. 23.   Chomsky has perhaps the same point in mind when he says that behaviouristic accounts of language learning fail to explain why we may not utter a word in the presence of the object and yet we do utter it in the absence of that object.
5 B.F. Skinner (1968), 'The Technology of Teaching' (New York, Appleton Century Crofts), p. 206.
6 Ibid., p. 5.

7   B.F. Skinner (1971), 'Beyond Freedom and Dignity'
    (London, Cape), p. 215.
8   D. Ingleby (1972), Ideology and the Human Sciences, in
    T. Pateman (ed.), 'Counter Course' (Harmondsworth,
    Penguin), p. 79.
9   I discuss this more fully in my book 'Problems in Primary
    Education' (1976, London, Routledge & Kegan Paul), ch. 2
    and in The Assessment of Learning, in 'British Journal of
    Educational Studies', vol. 27, no. 2, June 1979 (reprinted
    in this volume as chapter 10).
10 In chapter 32.
11 B.F. Skinner, 'Beyond Freedom and Dignity', op. cit.,
    p. 169.
12 See H. Sockett (1972), Curriculum Aims and Objectives,
    in 'Proceedings of the Philosophy of Education Society',
    vol. 6, no. 1, 1972.
13 See C. Clark (1979), Education and Behaviour Modification,
    in 'Journal of Philosophy of Education', vol. 13.

Part four
PRIMARY EDUCATION - PLOWDEN AND AFTER

12 REFLECTIONS ON PLOWDEN

THE 'PLOWDEN PHILOSOPHY'

Looking back at it some 'ten years on', I think that the Plowden Report must rank as the most interesting book on primary
education that I have ever read.   Admittedly, this is a field
where reading is more apt to be compulsory than compulsive.
And it is no easy task to find that golden mean between minutiae without perspective and romantic dreams which say more
about the dreamer than the reality which he ought to be
trying to comprehend.   But to see how near Plowden came to
the ideal, one need only compare it with earlier versions in
the history of the genre.   It had comprehensiveness of scope,
theoretical underpinning, an awareness of schooling realities
and a distinctive philosophy to offer.   It appeared at a time
of ferment when shape and guidance were unusually welcome.

But even though all of this may be true, that is not to say
that the report can be regarded as being beyond all criticism,
or as deserving unconditional acceptance, or as having found
limited support only through ignorance or misunderstanding of
its wisdom.   To acknowledge its great interest is not necessarily to agree with all of it.   There was much in it both of
great interest and also possibly right which I have no space
to comment upon: home/school relations and parental involvement;   the pursuit of that elusive goal 'equality of opportunity' through educational priority areas and the idea of 'positive discrimination';   the new concept of the 'middle school',
which in the event may be a junior school with a further year
uncertainly tacked on, or an institution with a quite new curricular and organisational structure;   and much more.

The part of the report on which I would like specifically to
focus here is Part Five, referred to by the committee as 'the
heart of the report'.   This was where the distinctive 'Plowden
philosophy' was to be found which was said to be a quickening
trend already emerging in the best schools.   What was this
distinctive 'Plowden philosophy', how has it fared and how
adequate can it be regarded today?   If we take first the
question of what it was, then I think that the best route to
an answer lies in asking in turn what was to be learned, how
the learner was conceived and what the role of the teacher
was thought to be.   And in placing learning before teaching

we not only have logic on our side but we also follow the clear order of priority emphasised in the report itself.

What the children were to learn in the Plowden school was to be selected and given its value by the children's own felt interests.   These interests in turn were to be elicited and guided by a stimulating environment of materials, plants, animals and visits selected and arranged by the teacher.   This resulted in a certain conception of an 'integrated curriculum' though a more accurate description of it would have been 'undifferentiated' since there was no putting together out of some prior separation but rather a refusal to separate at all: 'we stress that children's learning does not fit into subject categories' (555).

There was also a vague reference to a need for 'balance' and one chapter explicitly devoted to a discussion of the traditional subjects, but just how these two things were to be harmonised with the leading role of interests was never satisfactorily made clear.

The child himself as learner was conceived as being richly endowed with curiosity, interests and a general desire to learn.   He was seen as learning best through play, discovery, self-chosen and self-paced activity.   The guiding hand of Piaget led the committee to write: 'The child is the agent in his own learning' (529).   That is to say, the child actively constructs his knowledge and understanding out of his own active experience in a manner appropriate to his stage of development.   And the 'distinction between work and play is false' (523).

The teacher for his part would do a certain amount of group and class work but mainly his work would be with individuals. The nature of that work would be facilitatory: helping, advising, discussing, leading from behind as the children followed divergent paths of discovery.   The teacher's role was very far from being diminished in importance.   Indeed, this child-centred philosophy 'needs teachers of great personal qualities, strong character and a deep understanding of children, and it needs first-rate organisation' (739).   He had to be alert for signs of 'readiness', though it was uncertain readiness for what and this stage was admitted to be very difficult to spot. He had to be equipped with theories of child development deriving from Froebel but seen as amplified and confirmed by Piaget.   The 'Plowden philosophy' was a child-centred one. As such, it was not in general terms a new philosophy, and novelty of that kind was not claimed.

What was all of this set against?   The target was 'formal' teaching which sharply divided learning into separate subjects.

More than that, what was attacked was a picture of children
as learning best by sitting and listening to a teacher-instruc-
tor who required them collectively to switch their attention as
the bell and the timetable required.   The argument was
against an overemphasis on the 3 R's pursued by the 3 ups:
sit up, look up and shut up.   The message was plain in the
interesting list of 'danger signs' by reference to which we
might recognise when a school is going badly wrong: frequent
use of punishments, no changes in the last decade, much time
spent on teaching.   It has been remarked before that out of
thirty-six pictures of learning situations a teacher was visible
in only three.   Unremarked yet possibly even more significant
was that teaching aids appeared on the walls in only two pictures, almost all the space being devoted to the expressive
results of children's activity.

How widespread has the 'Plowden philosophy' become?   Did
the 'quickening trend' fully emerge?   Over ten years it has
been increasingly criticised, attacked and even ridiculed.
Black Papers and sections of the press have had a field day.
Spokesmen representing the authentic voice of all sound tradition have regularly been wheeled out at conferences to regale
their audiences with anecdotes supposedly illustrative of its
insanity.   Parents have been reliably reported as removing
their children down the road away from Plowden schools, or
else as launching compensatory programmes at home to remedy
the deficiencies of a poor school back-ground. (1)

If one looks for hard figures, Neville Bennett's twelve teaching styles could be regarded as covering Plowden teachers
with styles one and two.   In the north-west where Bennett
did his research, those two styles accounted for only 17 per
cent of his sample. (2)   But much more important than any
such figures was the way in which the Plowden philosophy
came to be seen as the 'official' theory.   It was what you
were smiled upon or promoted for.   It was what you were
sent on courses to discuss and learn about, or sent on visits
to other schools to see (perhaps tagging along behind crowds
of Americans).   In this way the report had an influence going
far beyond the relatively small band of its fully convinced and
fully understanding admirers.

CONTENT

Let us return to the question of the proper content of children's learning - a crucial matter on which to reach a decision
in any institution that can properly regard itself as a 'school'.
I think it is fair to say that Plowden rested its main weight
here on just one principle of curricular selection: the principle that there should be a certain desirable *attitude* towards

whatever was learned.   This attitude was one characterised
by interest above all, but one which could be more fully specified in terms of eagerness to learn, enjoyment, choice, self-
direction and in general control over one's own learning.

Certainly this is one very important aim of education.   If
we are truly to educate and not just superficially to inform,
then part of our endeavour will be to accomplish a personal
integration of what is learned which cannot be accomplished
without emotional involvement and actively 'making one's own'.
But *what* is learned is not therefore a matter of relative indif-
ference.   And Plowden's chapter on subjects is not a satisfactorily harmonised supplement to the dominant emphasis on
interest and discovery.   Questions of balance, sequence and
practice are not squarely faced.   There is an unjustified expectation of smooth and continuous development out of already
felt interests.   But an interest in Manchester United, Bionic
Woman or Gary Glitter is an inauspicious foundation on which
to construct a more than mean education.   Many interests are
socially determined and therefore reflect the merits or otherwise of the social influences which have been at work.   Why
should the teacher not number himself among such influences
and seek to engender quite new interests e.g. in a weather
station, in odd, even and prime numbers or in the vision of
birds?   To say that none of this would be ruled out overlooks
the fact that justice has not been done to the teacher's selection of material and choice of direction in which to 'develop'
an interest.

If we try to make the teacher's judgement here more explicit,
then at least two further principles of curricular selection
would have to be seen properly at work.   One of these is the
old liberal idea of a balanced general education, possibly specified in terms of the subject curriculum though there are variations on that theme such as Hirst's. (3)   Once some content
has been given to that idea, then secondary curricular principles such as breadth and balance can begin to get some
application.

The second of these further principles is that of preparation
for life.   Plowden stated that 'one obvious purpose is to fit
children for the society into which they will grow up' (494),
though almost immediately the report went on to say that children should 'learn to live first and foremost as children and not
as future adults' (505).   But children are future adults.
And since a very obvious part of their future is in secondary
education the problem of predicting their future is not so insuperable as it might at first seem.   Society also has a legitimate interest in the rising generation, most obviously in its
being morally educated and its being economically self-support-
ing.

Curricular suggestions come from all directions: from children's felt interests, from tradition, from pressure groups and
even nowadays from prime ministers. I suggest that the
school can make at least an initial judgement on any such suggestion by posing four questions: (1) Does it provide opportunities to develop interests, give scope for choice and effect
a very desirable personal integration? (2) Does it usefully
contribute towards a balanced general education? (3) Does it
usefully contribute to a preparation for life, so far as we can
reliably foresee it? (4) Is it best learned in school at all,
since not everything desirable can be included in the curriculum? The answers may sometimes pull in different directions
and no doubt should be differently weighted at different ages
and stages, but at least an overall perspective is provided
which can reveal gross omissions and imbalances. (4)

LEARNING BY DISCOVERY

A second aspect of the heart of the report was its emphasis
on learning by discovery. The committee even went on later
to say that 'finding out' has proved to be better for children
than 'being told' (1233). Had they *proved* that? It is not
even true without heavy qualification, but the assertion was
entirely in harmony with their one-sided emphasis on attitudinal aims. But consider the perspective in which discovery
learning is seen from an equally one-sided emphasis on preparation for life. Seen in that way such learning will appear
as slow, uncertain and inefficient, and impatience will lead to
the assertion that children learn faster and more reliably from
instruction, demonstration and practice. Thus each side
neglects what the other values by ignoring an important aim.

Some of the qualifications which need to be added to any
approval of discovery learning were discussed in the first
volume of 'Education 3-13'. But something further needs to
be said about certain important assumptions made by those
using discovery methods. For example, there are assumptions
about learners. It is assumed (sometimes justifiably) that the
learner already has sufficient related knowledge to see the
problem or to register the interest which it is hoped will
engage his attention. For example, at least some knowledge
of optics is probably necessary to pose to oneself as a problem
the relationship between observer, sun and object when we see
a rainbow.

A further assumption made about the learner is that he has,
or will soon spontaneously acquire, certain qualities of character (a much neglected aspect of the person both in the report
and elsewhere). Unwilled absorption is supposed to do all,
yet discovery learning frequently requires perseverance and

concentration if distractions are to be brushed aside, setbacks
are to be overcome and the tedious patches are to be worked
through.   How much easier and more tempting it is to wander
off out of sight somewhere or to become what Bruner has mem-
orably called a 'cruiser'.   There *is* a distinction between
work and play, as children themselves know well enough.
There is also some truth in the criticism that the Plowden
Report overgeneralised methods which may be highly appropriate in the nursery school but which are increasingly less
appropriate as the curriculum deepens in intellectual content.

A final point about learners is that they come to school very
differently prepared to cue in to what is required by a discovery approach.   This means that equality of opportunity to
succeed under this regime is seriously compromised from the
start.   It has even been suggested that talk of stages and
readiness provides the teacher with an excuse when confronted
by many children's failure to profit from this approach. (5)
However, it might be said on the other side that *any* approach
is inevitably going to distribute advantages and disadvantages
differentially.

Yet other assumptions are made about teachers and subject-
matter.   For example, the teacher is capable of organising
resources and keeping track of children who 'singly, or in
groups, follow divergent paths of discovery' (544).   He has
to have knowledge to identify genuine discoveries (which imply
truth) and to see lines of worthwhile development.   Clearly
the committee felt a strain in their proposals here, as is evident from their recommendations concerning 'consultant
teachers' who would embody the principle and advantages of
subject specialism without the disadvantages of timetabled
subject specialist teaching.

Concerning subject matter, the use of discovery methods
calls for a sharp sensitivity to what *can* be discovered.
Simple points of fact, particularly if they are true only
because of a social convention, are often best told if they are
not known by the child.   It is those facts into which rational
insight is possible which provide the most rewarding lines of
self-directed inquiry.   Then the possible gains from discovery
methods of intrinsic motivation and of developing powers of
self-direction are that much more likely.   But research seems
to indicate that there is no superiority, contrary to what is
often claimed, in terms of understanding and retention.

ASSESSMENT

A third aspect of Part Five of the report was its neglect of
assessment.   Although there are many incidental references

to this topic, there is no chapter or major section on it.
Mention is made of keeping records, especially in the form of
a folder of selected work.   Two-way reports to parents are
discussed, as is feedback from secondary schools.   A place
is found for standardised tests, for national surveys of attainment and for ten-yearly surveys by HMIs.   But day-by-day
assessment in the form of marking, systematic observation,
testing and general checking-up is neglected.   The importance of seeing that children learn and of monitoring what
they are learning does not get the attention that it deserves.
Bennett rightly made 'testing and grading' something which
the Plowden teacher typically discourages, (6) and 'concentration on tests' was another of the 'danger signs' (503).

Of course, measuring never increased anyone's height by so
much as an inch.   And no doubt comparative grading and
competitive orders of merit have many undesirable side-effects.
But that is to object only to certain *forms* of assessment.
The point of concern here has recently been forcefully stres-
sed by Antony Flew and it is simply this: anyone who is
serious about either teaching or learning ought to be interested in how far he is actually succeeding, whatever his 'teaching style'. (7)   How else is he to *know* that the level of difficulty is right, that work is now of a sufficient standard to
leave it and pass on and what it would be appropriate to do
next?   Vague impressions are not good enough.   We must
deliberately put ourselves in a position to learn of our mistakes and from our mistakes.

To some extent this can be accomplished by self-assessment,
which is of course more than simply keeping a record of work
done.   But there is an interesting absurdity in, for example,
a child hearing himself read.   Assessment involves appeal to
something independent of our first impressions.   So self-
assessment is intelligible where a child checks against answers,
compares his performance with a record or tape, consults a
work of reference or uses self-correcting apparatus.   In
these cases, although he may still be mistaken, there is a reference to something independent.   In many instances, however, for one reason or another the teacher will have to do
the checking up.   Actually *knowing* how you are doing is in-
dispensable to intelligent teaching and learning, as it is to
practice generally.   It is also secondarily important for motivation and for publicly available records of progress.

THE VIRTUE OF MODESTY

In these reflections on Plowden 'ten years on' I have concentrated on what the committee itself saw as the heart of the
report.   But I do have one final and more general reflection

of urgent topicality.   The Plowden Committee had great
advantages.   They drew on the evidence of hundreds of
experts, associations and witnesses.   They conducted national
surveys and visited Europe, USA and USSR.   They spent
thousands of pounds and recommended the spending of millions
more.   Yet ten years on many people would agree that they
failed to reach the final truth about primary education.
Indeed they modestly said that 'nobody will suppose that we
have now reached final truth' (2).   Others in close sympathy
with them were less modest. (8)

Where then should we be now if Plowden, with every advantage, had had the force of coercive central authority behind
it?   Ten years on there are voices less mindful of the virtue
of modesty where truth is concerned, and of diversity as a
means of slowly bringing it to light.

REFERENCES

1 Sharp, R., Green, A. and Lewis, J. (1973), 'Education and
  Social Control' (London, Routledge & Kegan Paul), p. 59
  and p. 208.
2 Bennett, N. (1976), 'Teaching Styles and Pupil Progress'
  (London, Open Books), p. 149.
3 See for instance, Dearden, R.F. (1968), 'Philosophy of
  Primary Education' (London, Routledge & Kegan Paul),
  ch. 4.
4 These and other questions are much more fully discussed in
  Dearden, R.F. (1976), 'Problems in Primary Education'
  (London, Routledge & Kegan Paul).
5 Sharp, Green and Lewis, op. cit.
6 Bennett, op. cit.
7 Flew, A. (1977), 'Sociology, Equality and Education', ch. 6.
8 See for example L. Marsh's approving quotation of Christian
  Schiller in Marsh, L. (1970), 'Alongside the Child' (London,
  Black), p. 1.

13 THE PRIMARY SURVEY: AN ASSESSMENT

First impressions of the Inspectorate's report on primary education may be false ones. (1)   For example, in December 1978
the editorial in 'Child Education' said that 'It is hard to know
what to make of the Inspectorate's report on "Primary Education in England" ... really the trouble with the report as a
whole [is that] it's not anything much.'   A generous way of
accounting for this unfavourable impression would be to see it
as an indirect tribute to Plowden.   For the Plowden Report of
1967 set new high standards.   It was comprehensive.   It
constantly interwove theory and practice.   It had memorable
keynote passages, such as the one containing the assertion
that 'the child is the agent in his own learning.'   This latest
report, by contrast, is intentionally limited in scope, and it
contains neither any explicit theory nor any purple passages.
One way of seeing it as related to Plowden, however, is to
see it as a response to Plowden's call (para. 290) for surveys
of the quality of primary education to be undertaken every ten
years.   But if by such 'quality' was intended a confirmation
of the spread of Plowden's own child-centred philosophy, then
this latest report cannot be seen as such a confirmation, for
reasons that will soon be apparent.

Of all people, the Inspectorate are in the best position to
report on the schools as a whole.   Not only do they as a
body cover the whole country, but they can also rely on co-
operation, as we see in the 99.6 per cent response rate to the
headteachers' long questionnaire (a response rate to my knowledge matched only by Soviet elections).   Their first and most
obvious finding is of very great political importance.   This is
that the schools have not 'abandoned the basics', standards
are not falling (except that of HMI's spelling in the first
printing), every other school is not a Tyndale and chaos does
not reign.   The angry censure to which primary schools
have recently been subjected, and the wild and evidently
baseless accusations that have been thrown at them by some
parents, by the press and by some politicians, can now be
confidently turned aside.   There is no need to 'get back to
the basics' and indeed schools do better if they pursue the
basics through a wide curriculum.   In fact, an opposite problem now looming up will be to protect the width of the curriculum in the face of contracting rolls and staff.

Then are there grounds for complacency?   Apparently
there are grounds for satisfaction where the less able 50 per
cent of pupils are concerned [as Chapter 1 points out].   The
work being done with these children is broadly as it should
be.   But the position with the more able is rather more disconcerting.   With these children there is indeed a problem.
And it is not just the problem which Plowden thought might
exist of adequately stretching the 'gifted', or the most able
5 per cent.   The report finds that the more able 50 per cent
are not being sufficiently stretched.   Their work is superficial, is not challenging, and it lacks progression.   Two general statements of this deficiency are the following:

8.33   *the more able children with a class were the least
       likely to be doing work that was sufficiently chal-
       lenging* [their italics]
8.67   the immediate aim ... should probably be to take what
       is done to greater depth rather than to introduce con-
       tent that is new to primary education.

Hints of a need for some intellectual stiffening regularly
appear.   Thus 'more could be done ... to encourage them to
follow a line of argument, to evaluate evidence, or to reach
judgements in the course of discussion.'

This general deficiency is particularised.   Thus the report
urges attention to advanced reading skills such as scanning,
skimming, interpreting, seeing implications and following arguments critically.   More difficult writing tasks are advocated
such as presenting a coherent argument, exploring alternative
possibilities, drawing conclusions and making judgements.   In
mathematics, more demanding work should be set rather than
further repetitive practice.   Science should go beyond the
present superficial level to more careful observation and accurate recording, the formulation of hypotheses and the testing
of them.   History should go beyond superficial copying from
reference books and lead towards an understanding of historical change and an awareness of the nature of historical evidence.   Similarly, geography should go beyond superficial
weather observations.

Earlier I remarked that this report is not just a confirmation
of the spread of 'quality' understood in the Plowden sense.
A significantly different educational philosophy is implicitly
contained in these suggestions.   Let part of paragraph 544
in Plowden serve as a reminder of what was sought in 1967:

The newer methods start with the direct impact of the envir-
onment on the child and the child's individual response to it.
The results are unpredictable but extremely worthwhile.
The teacher has to be prepared to follow up the personal

interest of the children who, either singly, or in groups,
follow divergent paths of discovery.... The teacher needs
perception to appreciate the value of what can be gained
from this method of working, and he needs also energy to
keep up with the children's demands.

Thus the Plowden stress was on 'spontaneous' interests, discovery, and following the lead of the child.

Now contrast some statements from the 1978 report:

8.25 *Curricular content should be selected not only to suit
the interests and abilities of the children and to provide for the progressive development of the basic
skills, but also because it is important in its own
right....* The teacher's need for a thorough knowledge of the subject becomes more marked as the children get older [their italics].
8.58 It is vital that teachers should be knowledgeable in
what they teach.

Here and elsewhere in the report the emphasis is unPlowden-
like. The importance of an ordered and progressive curriculum is assumed. There is to be the teaching of groups round
a blackboard. Special posts for curricular areas are recommended and special curricular strengths of staff are to be exploited. As rolls contract, freed rooms are seen in terms of
possible specialist purposes. Although specialist teaching on
the secondary school model is not advocated, there is the un-
mistakable impression of thinking from secondary practices
downwards rather than, as with Plowden, thinking from infant
school practices upwards.

This is not the place to raise once again the merits of the
Plowden philosophy. That is something which has been considered in detail and at length elsewhere. (2) (3) The context
in which the latest report places its change in philosophy is
one of social demands for rising levels of skill. Such a utilitarian conception, valid though it is, is not the only conception which might be invoked. Surely doing greater justice to
intellectual development can be justified also in terms of individual fulfilment and the realisation of worthwhile individual
powers and abilities? The more able children deserve to be
stretched quite apart from social utility. It may not be much
use to an employer if attention has been given to historical
change and evidence, or if in geography the work went
beyond simple weather observations, but such things are very
relevant to leading a more interesting and fully engaged life.
In short, something of the intentions behind the idea of a
liberal education can be appropriately invoked, though admittedly they may lack political cutting edge where narrow

counsels prevail.   Nevertheless, it is important that educators
should not forget what they are about, even if less generous
conceptions have to be relied upon in speaking to the world at
large.

I shall not comment further on the question of the general
justification for this implicit shift away from a Plowden philosophy, beyond venturing the opinion that in my view the
report is justified where junior and middle schools are concerned, in trying to effect such a shift.   There is, however,
another matter that calls for comment.   In spite of its insistence that greater attention should be given to the intellectual
development of the 50 per cent or so of more able children,
the report is really rather vague about what form that intellectual development should take.   Perhaps it was the proper
task of the report to do no more than to raise the level of
awareness of this problem, leaving to others and to other
sorts of occasion the working out of how the problem might be
solved.   Such a report admittedly cannot do everything itself,
but must be supplemented by local action in the way of sensi-
tising conferences, in-service courses, advisory programmes,
exchange visits between schools and so on.   But even at its
chosen level of generality, does the report rightly conceptualise the problem?   How, indeed, does it conceptualise it?

To judge from the passages quoted earlier in juxtaposition to
some passages from Plowden, it might be thought that a
greater emphasis on intellectual development would mean giving
more attention to the traditional range of curricular *subjects*.
The children, and presumably also their teachers, should
simply learn more about and deepen their understanding of
the usual range of subjects.   There are passages which do
suggest that this was what was meant, and it seems intelligible
and defensible enough.   Thus the report comments on the inadequacy of teaching children graphical methods of representing data only to the extent of teaching them how to construct
simple block graphs and then being content endlessly to vary
that one theme.   What more, then, might be wanted?   Suggestions are readily conceivable.   For example, the connection
with averages can be noted, and how the blocks above the
average line equal the spaces below it.   Line graphs can be
introduced and the characteristic discussed that every point
on the line must have significance, so making it necessary to
choose appropriately the form of graph to employ.   Axes can
be extended to negative values.   Misleading graphical displays, culled perhaps from newspapers, can be discussed.
Circular displays can be introduced, linking the work with
percentages and angular measure ... and so on.

To take another example, the report says that historical
work is deficient in that no attention is given to historical

change and the nature of historical evidence.   Is that an inappropriate secondary school conception?   A primary teacher
might, for example, duplicate copies of some pages of an early
local census return to serve as evidence.   On that basis,
such changes might be discussed as fashions in Christian
names, size of family, kinds of work, wives and work, schooling ages and geographical mobility.   Links with other subjects (something much advocated in the report) might be
sought through the use of maps, associated computations and
the introduction of the idea of a possible sampling error in
generalising from such limited evidence.   In ways such as
these, greater intellectual development can be seen to involve
not just more information but critical attention to evidence,
discussion of its possible significance or interpretation, and
setting the matter in a wider context of understanding.   In
these and other ways the older and more able children can
begin more fully to enter into the possession of their potential
intellectual powers.

For suggestions such as these to be practicable, it may well
be that secondary practice should be copied at least to the
extent of allowing primary teachers more free time for the
preparation and following up of work in the classroom.   This
is one possibility presented by contracting rolls which the
report does not much discuss, though at some future time
people may well look back and wonder how teachers were ever
expected to sustain such a highly professional level of imaginative activity throughout a whole day without breaks for
planning, preparation of materials, collecting data and the
like.   But such practical difficulties apart, the work envisaged would at least be acceptably conceptualised.

There is, however, an alternative conception which regularly
surfaces throughout the report.   In this conception, intellectual development is thought of as a developing of certain
apparently quite general *skills*.   For example, there is a
whole section entitled 'learning to notice and to think' (5.10-
5.13).   In that section, children are envisaged as 'learning to
notice relevant features'.   Elsewhere, a new basic skill makes
its appearance, namely 'comprehension' (6.5), and children
are to be taught 'to comprehend the main ideas in information
given to them'.   At 5.21, 'listening skills' appear and at 5.47
reading skills such as 'the capacity to make sense of difficult
passages'.   At 5.72, we are urged to 'teach children how to
make careful observations', because 'in science it is essential
that children should develop observational skills and begin to
recognise similarities and differences' (5.70).   'Observing
skill' is returned to in the final chapter where it is said that
*Intending primary school teachers should be helped to recog-
nise the importance of teaching children to observe carefully,
encouraging them to try to explain what they have noticed and
to test their explanations*' (8.56, their italics).

This conception of intellectual development is, to put it
mildly, highly controversial.   In the philosophy of education
it is debated under the title 'general powers of the mind', the
question at issue being whether there can be such *general*
powers. (4)   Can there be such general skills as skill in
noticing, observing skill, thinking skill, comprehension skill
or listening skill?   If there cannot be, then effort will be
misdirected in trying to improve primary education in pursuit
of such skills and related in-service training will be wrongly
focused.   The question is therefore no 'merely academic' one,
or a matter 'just of semantics'.   The question has a long history which goes back to faculty psychology and the idea that
certain subjects, such as Latin, could train the general mental
powers and so make us fit for any specific future task.
Reasoning, memory, judgement, imagination, will and observation each had its appropriate muscle-developing exercises.

Certainly there can be skills of general application.   It
would be very surprising if this were not so, since otherwise
why should we class activities together and call them by the
same name?   For example, across all the varieties of subject
for discussion, there are some generally relevant observances,
such as listening to what others say, contributing relevantly
and separating oneself from the substance of the view put forward for discussion.   But such skills (if skill is the right
word) will not be sufficient for the discussion to be a good
one, since for that to happen the participants must also be
knowledgeable in the subject matter under discussion.   The
same point could be made about a supposed general 'interview-
ing skill' of the sort that television trainees might be given.
There would indeed be common elements of skill in approach-
ing interviewees, but also needed would be some specific knowledge of the subject matter of the interview.   So commonly is
this lacking that in practice we all too often witness fatuous
questions, or no capacity to follow up a reply, or no awareness of standard objections to what is said.   The general
skills are not sufficient.

The same points can be made about the report's supposed
general skills.   There may indeed be something in common to
all occasions of listening (paying attention for example) but
specific knowledge is needed if we are to listen to (or for)
the reed-warbler, the wrong engine valve-setting, the rhythm
of the poetic line, the minor key, the Frenchman's message,
the scientific explanation or the note of regret.   'General
listening skill', if there is such a thing, would be rather
trivial by comparison with specifics here.   Much the same
goes for general 'observing skill'.   What we observe is relative to our knowledge and interests.   The sharpest of hedge-
row observers may still fail to notice that his wife has had her
hair done, and the keenest follower of the detail design differ-

ences in the latest marks of cars may be blind to pattern in
the landscape.　Much the same points would need to be made
about any supposed general 'thinking skill' or 'problem-solving
skill'.　And what on earth is a general (or 'basic') comprehension skill supposed to consist of?　Where there is generality, then let us by all means draw attention to it and so anticipate whole classes of future experiences;　but at the same
time let us also recognise that 'skills' can become a mindless
incantation serving only to render vague what we should be
seeking to teach.

Two powerful pressures push towards the 'general skills'
conception of intellectual development, though mistakenly.
These are the explosion in knowledge and the obsolescence of
knowledge.　There is too much knowledge and what we learn
of it may cease to be useful.　If we could find some more
economically learned and more permanently valuable general
skills, then they would indeed constitute golden knowledge
... if such skills existed.　Certainly some accommodation to
these pressures is possible.　We can teach children how to
find out what they do not know (provided that this source of
information will be comprehensible when it is located).　We
can teach the methodology of a subject, where there is one.
And the particular can be milked of as much generality as it
will yield.　But in order to see that all of this will fall far
short of the dream, consider a supposed general teaching
skill.　Rather than train teachers to teach mathematics, or
art, or physical education, or music, or religion, or biology,
should we instead go for 'general teaching skill'?　There
would indeed be something to learn, but would it be sufficient?
Can a sixth-form history teacher be put straight into a nursery class?　Can a junior school teacher take over a university seminar on the Icelandic sagas or new techniques in den-
tistry?

I take the answers to be obvious.　If by 'listening skill' is
meant no more than that children should pay attention when
their teachers explain something, or if by 'observing skill' is
meant noticing certain particular sorts of feature to which in
one way or another attention is drawn, then there is no objection.　Something rather specific is then being referred to in
a misleadingly over-general way.　And the fault of the report
here might arguably be no more than that.　But I think a
rather deeper misconception is at work, which makes important
practical differences.　For example, if the more able 50 per
cent need only to acquire certain general skills, such as
noticing skill, then in-service courses and other sorts of help
for teachers will seem unnecessary.　Just get the children to
'notice' more.　But if the intellectual development sought is
by way of, for example, a deepened understanding of science
(which will of course include some specific *problem-related*

observing, listening, comprehending, etc.) then both teachers
and taught will need to know or to learn some science.

What I have been suggesting about the latest HMI report is
as follows.   The report should perform a valuable political
function in getting ill-informed and sensationalist critics off
the backs of the primary schools.   Where the less able half
of primary children are concerned, the schools are doing well,
as they are with all children in the elementary parts of the
traditional basic subjects.   But the report is not mere confirmation of the spread of Plowden's ideas.   It somewhat departs
from Plowden's child-centred philosophy more towards a sub-
ject-centred view.   However, this departure is not a return
to fact-cramming or the rote learning of blocks of information,
but an advocacy of stimulating intellectual development.   How
is that to be conceived?   Here the report is unclear as to
what it wants, and unclear in ways which could compromise
choosing the right targets for in-service help.   My own suggestion is that intellectual development should be conceived as
a deepening critical awareness of subjects along the lines
earlier illustrated with reference to mathematics and history.
The alternative conception as developing a set of quite general
skills is largely a misconception, since even where there is
such generality it is often trivial, and it is never sufficient.

REFERENCES

1 Department of Education and Science (1978), 'Primary Education in England: A Survey by HM Inspectors of Schools'
   (London, HMSO).
2 'Education 3-13' (1978), vol. 6, no. 1 (reprinted in this
   volume as chapter 12).
3 Peters, R. (ed.), (1969), 'Perspectives on Plowden'
   (London, Routledge & Kegan Paul).
4 Brown, S. (ed.) (1975), 'Philosophers Discuss Education'
   (London, Macmillan), part two.

INDEX